Connecting Your Students with the World

Make the most of today's technology to give your students a more interactive, authentic learning experience! *Connecting Your Students with the World* shows you how to use web tools to get K–8 students in touch with other classrooms worldwide. This book is a valuable resource to help you find and communicate with other teachers and classrooms and even design your own collaborative online projects. You'll find out how to:

♦ Conduct videoconferencing calls to put your students in touch with classrooms around the world;
♦ Embark on Virtual Field Trips;
♦ Plan themed projects for every season, including fun holiday activities;
♦ And more!

The book includes detailed instructions for each activity and connections to the Common Core, ISTE, and Next Generation Science Standards, so you can ensure that you are meeting your state's requirements as you prepare your students to become engaged, informed, and global citizens. Additionally, a comprehensive list of online resources is available as a free download from the Routledge resource at www.routledge.com/books/details/9781138902961

Billy Krakower (@wkrakower) is the Computer Technology Instructor and Gifted & Talented Teacher for grades 3 and 4 at Beatrice Gilmore Elementary School in the Woodland Park Public School District, Woodland Park, New Jersey.

Paula Naugle (@plnaugle) is a fourth-grade English language arts and social studies teacher at a suburban public school near New Orleans.

Jerry Blumengarten (@cybraryman1) is the creator of Cybrary Man's Educational Web Sites, which started as a school library website and is now used by educators all over the world.

Other Eye on Education Books
Available from Routledge
(www.routledge.com/eyeoneducation)

What Connected Educators Do Differently
Todd Whitaker, Jeffrey Zoul, and Jimmy Casas

Close Reading in Elementary School
Bringing Readers and Texts Together
Diana Sisson and Betsy Sisson

Inquiry and Innovation in the Classroom
Using 20% Time, Genius Hour, and PBL to Drive Student Success
A.J. Juliani

The Passion-Driven Classroom
A Framework for Teaching and Learning
Angela Maiers and Amy Sandvold

The Common Core Grammar Toolkit
Using Mentor Texts to Teach the Language Standards in Grades 3–5
Sean Ruday

The Common Core Grammar Toolkit
Using Mentor Texts to Teach the Language Standards in Grades 6–8
Sean Ruday

Nonfiction Strategies That Work
Do This—Not That!
Lori G. Wilfong

Writing Strategies That Work
Do This—Not That!
Lori G. Wilfong

Vocabulary Strategies That Work
Do This—Not That!
Lori G. Wilfong

The Educator's Guide to Writing a Book
Practical Advice for Teachers and Leaders
Cathie E. West

Reinventing Writing
The 9 Tools That Are Changing Writing, Teaching, and Learning Forever
Vicki Davis

Connecting Your Students with the World

Tools and Projects to Make Global
Collaboration Come Alive, K-8

Billy Krakower, Paula Naugle, and Jerry Blumengarten

 Routledge
Taylor & Francis Group

NEW YORK AND LONDON

First published 2016
by Routledge
711 Third Avenue, New York, NY 10017

and by Routledge
2 Park Square, Milton Park, Abingdon, Oxon, OX14 4RN

Routledge is an imprint of the Taylor & Francis Group, an informa business

Library of Congress Cataloging-in-Publication Data
Krakower, Billy.
    Connecting your students with the world : tools and projects to make
global collaboration come alive, K-8 / by Billy Krakower, Paula Naugle,
and Jerry Blumengarten.
        pages cm
    Includes bibliographical references.
    1. Internet in education.   2. Communication in education.   3. Group
work in education.   4. Education, Elementary—Activity programs
I. Naugle, Paula.   II. Blumengarten, Jerry.   III. Title.
    LB1044.87.K73 2016
    371.33'44678—dc23
    2015012194

ISBN: 978-1-138-90295-4 (hbk)
ISBN: 978-1-138-90296-1 (pbk)
ISBN: 978-1-315-69720-8 (ebk)

Typeset in Palatino
by Apex CoVantage, LLC

Printed and bound in the United States of America by Publishers Graphics,
LLC on sustainably sourced paper.

Billy:
To my wife, Jennifer, who has been there for me during
the writing of the book as a sounding board and supporter.
To my PLN, whom I learn and grow with every day.

Paula:
To my companion, Robert Weems, whose abundant patience
has been truly appreciated. To all the members of my
PLN, without whom my journey to global collaboration
would not have happened. Thank you for your
constant encouragement and inspiration.

Jerry:
To my wife, Gail; children, Neil and Shira; grandchildren
Madison, Sam, Olivia, Jackson, Ada; and my awesome
global PLN, who inspire me every day.

From all:
To our PLN, thank you from the bottom of our hearts for
all the input you have given us and the collaborative
projects you have done with us. Without your
collaboration this book would not exist.

Contents

eResources

A hyperlinked list of the online resources mentioned in this book is available on our website. To download, go to the book product page, www.routledge.com/books/details/9781138902961. Then click on the "eResources" tab and select the file. The document will begin downloading to your device.

Meet the Authors

Billy Krakower (@wkrakower) is a full-time teacher at Woodland Park Public Schools in Woodland Park, New Jersey, where he has taught computers and special education to grades 3 and 4 for over eight years. He is the Chief Financial and Event Officer for Evolving Educators, LLC (www.evolvingeducators.com). Billy co-moderates two weekly Twitter chats: #NJed chat and #satchat (for educational leaders). He co-hosts *SatChat Radio*, a weekly show interviewing educators on BAM Radio Network and available on iTunes. Billy is one of the lead organizers of Edcamp New Jersey and EdcampLeadership North NJ. He is on the teacher advisory board for ReadWorks. Billy is a 2014 ASCD Emerging Leader, is a member of the NJASCD executive board, and serves as the technology committee chair. He also served as co-director of NJASCD Northern Region (Fall 2013–June 2015). He has presented at more than 20 local and national technology conferences on topics including Twitter & You, The Science Behind a Mystery Location Call, and Connecting Beyond the Classroom.

Billy has an Advanced Certificate in Educational Leadership and a dual master's degree in Special Education and Elementary Education from Long Island University. Billy is a Google Certified Educator and an Edmodo Certified Trainer. You can read more about Billy, his awards, and his presentations at www.billykrakower.com. He is passionate about helping every child and adult enjoy and learn using technology tools in easy, fun, and empowering ways.

Paula Naugle is a veteran classroom teacher with over 35 years of experience. She earned her master's degree from Southeastern Louisiana University in Educational Technology Leadership. She currently teaches fourth graders English language arts and social studies at Bissonet Plaza Elementary School, which is a suburban public school near New Orleans.

Integrating technology into her lessons is a passion for Paula. She received a $15,000 technology grant from her district, which allowed her to add many technology tools to her classroom. Currently she is updating her classroom computers with DonorsChoose grants. She has her students connecting and collaborating with other students around the globe on projects using web tools such as Skype, Google Hangouts, Edmodo, Google Docs, TodaysMeet, and many more.

Paula is a connected educator and uses social media to pursue her own professional development on a daily basis. She is a Discovery Educator Network (DEN) STAR, a DEN Leadership Council member for Louisiana, a Microsoft Innovative Educator, a Simple K12 Ambassador, a co-founder and moderator for #4thchat, an Edcamp NOLA organizer, an Edmodo Ambassador and certified trainer, and a PBworks certified trainer. She is on the teacher advisory boards for TeachersFirst, Classroom 2.0 Live, and ReadWorks.

Paula has presented at all levels (locally, statewide, nationally, and internationally) both in person and virtually. She has presented for ISTE (2011, 2012, 2014, 2015), Louisiana Association of Computer Using Educators (LACUE) Conference (2009, 2010, 2011, 2012, 2013, 2014, 2015), Discovery Education, Intel, BrainPOP, Simple K12, various Edcamps and TeachMeets, the SITE International Conference, Reform Symposium Virtual Conference, Classroom 2.0 Live, the K12 Online Conference, and more. In 2012 she was invited to attend the Midwest Educational Technology Conference (METC) as a featured presenter. Some of her many presentation topics include Global Collaboration, Being a Connected Educator, Mystery Location Calls, Edmodo, Blogging with Elementary Students, Google Tips and Tricks, and Being Better at Math.

Paula was born in New York state, was educated in Pennsylvania, and has taught in the state of Louisiana since she moved there in 1977. Her hobbies include traveling, reading, and learning about the latest tech tools that can be used in her classroom.

Jerry Blumengarten, also known as Cybrary Man, is a constant learner who is a champion of front-line educators who do their best to facilitate the learning of all students. He considers himself a Twitterbrarian who is attempting to curate the Internet for educators, students, and parents. Jerry joyfully serves as a moderator on #edchat. He has guest-moderated many other Twitter educational chats and created #engsschat. He has been a featured speaker at #METC13 and #GaETC13 and given keynotes and presentations at 15 Edcamps and TeachMeets. At ISTE he has given workshops and presentations and served on panels. He also is a commentator on BAM Radio.

Jerry taught for 32 years in the New York City school system. He worked in four inner-city middle schools in Brooklyn, for the first 20 years mainly as a social studies teacher, but he taught most subject areas and for the final 12 years he served as a teacher-librarian. He also helped coach two different schools to back-to-back city track championships. He wrote curriculum for his school district, the New York City Board of Education, and Open Doors, a School-Business Partnership. He also wrote over 35 booklets on the environment, safety, careers, and water, electrical, and gas safety for the Culver Company, a leader in supplying educational materials for the utility industry. He served on the executive board of the Association of Teachers of Social Studies, was very active in the National Council for the Social Studies (NCSS) presenting sessions, and served as chairperson of the Urban Social Studies Education Committee.

The middle school library site he created has morphed into Cybrary Man's Educational Web Sites, which has information on most subject areas for all grade levels. Jerry was a pioneer in the use of technology during his school career.

While living on Long Island he was elected several times to the town's library board. On Cape Cod he was elected as a charter commissioner and helped write a town charter that was approved. Jerry has his BA degree with a major in Political Science from the University of Pittsburgh and an MA degree in the Teaching of Social Studies from Hunter College, City University of New York.

On Twitter Jerry can be found as @cybraryman1.

Our Story

The three of us live in different parts of the United States and have an amazing story about the ways in which this book came to fruition.

Paula started doing Mystery Skype Calls back in 2009. Once Google Hangouts became available for videoconferencing in the classroom, she suggested to the online community through her blog that Mystery Skype Calls become known as Mystery Location Calls.

Billy started doing Mystery Skype Calls in 2012. His first-ever call was with Nancy Carroll right after the New York Giants and the New England Patriots got into the Super Bowl. After their first Mystery Skype Call, Nancy and Billy discussed how they could further expand a Mystery Skype.

On September 13, 2012, the initial #4thchat Google Hangout began. Educators from seven states began meeting each week to connect, collaborate, and share ideas on how to best facilitate learning for students. Most of them had never met each other in person. The group consists of Billy Krakower (@wkrakower) from New Jersey, Jerry Blumengarten (@cybraryman1) from Florida, Jessica Bamberger (@MissBamberger) from Pennsylvania, Kim Powell (@kimpowelledtech) from Michigan, Paula Naugle (@plnaugle) from Louisiana, Nancy Carroll (@ncarroll24) from Massachusetts, Jennifer Regruth (@JennRegruth) from Indiana, and periodically Dan Curcio (@dandanscience) and Jeff Bradbury (@TeacherCast) from New Jersey.

The Sunday Night Google Hangout group still meets on a regular basis to discuss different collaborative ideas and projects they can do with their classrooms. They share ideas that others can use and just discuss all things education. While on these Google Hangouts they frequently work on Google Docs at the same time. They have become a close family and are excited to share their projects with others on Twitter and other social media outlets, such as Voxer and Google+.

Their panel titled "Anytime, Anyplace, Anywhere: Taking Charge of Your Own PD" was accepted for ISTE 2015.

Billy first met Paula at ISTE 2011 in Philadelphia, Pennsylvania. Little did they know theirs would soon blossom into an amazing collaborative relationship. Paula started telling people about #4thchat and how they could connect with other educators across the country. Soon Billy started to join Twitter chats. At first, like so many others, he was only lurking and watching. It was after a conversation with Kevin Jarrett at the New Jersey Education Association Teacher Convention that he really decided to get involved and participate in #4thchat. After Billy met Jerry at Edcamp SS in the spring of 2012, he started other Twitter chats, such as #NJed and #satchat.

Jerry and Paula had their first face-to-face meeting at ISTE 2012 in San Diego, California. They had known each other online, so meeting in real life was like a reunion for them. They now have an even stronger relationship.

Billy, Paula, and Jerry decided to put in a proposal for a workshop at ISTE 2014 in Atlanta, Georgia. Their workshop was accepted and was titled "Connecting Your Students to Collaborate with the World." The workshop was focused on Mystery Location/Skype Calls. They had their participants, who consisted of teachers and administrators, run through a typical call. This experience gave the participants a real taste of how they can do these calls with the students in their schools.

Billy and Jerry joined Paula and many others from their personal learning network (PLN) and have been presenting on this topic at local, state, national, and international conferences. In this book, they will look at other ways in which to use Google Hangouts and Skype beyond the actual Mystery Location Call. You will learn about different collaborative project ideas that can be used to connect more than one classroom at a time. These projects can all be linked to the Common Core State Standards or your state's standards. Examples of projects that have been successfully used by the authors are collaboration on math surveys, science experiments, Virtual Field Trips, Read Across America Day, and the Olympic Game Show Quiz. This book will discuss the ways in which these projects have been organized and planned and give you the details on how to implement these projects in your classroom.

Acknowledgments

The genesis of this book came from the fact that we are connected educators who passionately see the need to connect our students to collaborate with the world. Paula, Billy, and Jerry originally got together as a result of their activity on Twitter. It took a few years but we met each other at educational conferences. On Twitter we came together on #4thchat and started a weekly Google Hangout to generate ideas on ways to connect classes and collaborate. We would especially like to thank our Sunday Night Google Hangout group: Jessica Bamberger, Nancy Carroll, Dan Curcio, Kim Powell, and Jennifer Regruth.

Thank you for sharing your stories of collaboration with us and allowing us to include them in our book: Meghan Everette, Melissa Butler, Dennis Dill, Patti Grayson, Kevin Jarrett, Todd LaVogue, Elissa Malespina, Diana Rendina, Dr. Mark Salemi, Jennifer Wagner, and Linda Yollis.

How to Use This Book

This book is meant to be used as a practical guide for "Connecting Students to the World." We, as educators, want you to be able to use this book as a how-to guide and refer to it for ideas and ways to connect. It is hoped that you will take advantage of the amazing collaborative tools that are available in the digital age to facilitate the learning of children. We highly recommend as an initial activity using a **Mystery Location Call**, but you should feel free to use any of the ideas in this book to begin with. In the book we have gone into a lot of detail on how to prepare your students for a Mystery Location Call. We have used our own experiences as well as those of many other teachers who have successfully connected their students using this method. Please feel free to adapt the ideas we have given you to suit your own students and classrooms. We hope that you find this book a valuable resource as you start connecting your students to collaborate with the world.

We have made suggestions for all of our projects on which **Common Core State Standards** (www.ccsso.org/Resources/Programs/), **ISTE Standards** for both teachers and students, and **Next Generation Science Standards (NGSS)** would apply (see Appendix B for more information on the **ISTE** [International Society of Technology in Education] Standards). There is a table at the beginning of each project listing the standards' correlation along with a correlation chart in the back of the book with each project and standard. Depending on how you work these suggested projects with your students, you could add other standards as well.

Please note that the **bold-faced** words (the first time they appear in the book) can be found in the glossary.

1

Connecting Your Students

Be Connected—Be Engaged—Be Informed

Many of today's classroom teachers know the importance of being **connected educators** and the fact that we should be modeling for our students how to become connected and be responsible global citizens. It is necessary, however, to have more of our teacher colleagues connected so that they can network with passionate educators all around the world. This will better facilitate the learning of the children we serve. We have grown as educators through our presence on **Twitter**. We have built strong global **PLN**s (personal or professional learning networks) that have enabled us to connect, share, and learn with passionate teachers, administrators, community members, and parents, as well as others interested in education. It has also provided us with the opportunity to connect our students with the world. With our students, however, we struggle to try to make these connections while covering the standards and preparing our students for the myriad of testing that is commonplace in most schools today. How can we fit it all together and make it work?

We will describe how the projects contained in our book can cover a multitude of standards, enabling today's teachers to weave it all together in a way that is engaging, fun, and meaningful for our students as they prepare for their global futures.

Figure 1.1 E-Mail Around the World Project.

In the "dark ages" of the 1950s and 1960s we reached out to others outside our classrooms via telephones whose lines were connected to wall outlets and by mailing letters. The picture-postcard exchanges decorated bulletin boards and allowed us to correspond with the world outside the classroom walls. The 1970s and 1980s saw the beginning of the use of online message boards to communicate. The **Email Around the World** project in the late 1990s produced wonderful exchanges from faraway places (www.cybraryman.com/email.html). The **Flat Stanley** exchange began late in the 1990s and early 2000s and allowed classes to connect with one another via mail. However, what was lacking was a more personalized, "in the moment" exchange.

Connecting the Old-Fashioned Way

It is wonderful that technology enables us to connect easily and in the moment without having to wait. After the tech connection, though, it is nice to continue by resorting to the tried-and-true old-fashioned ways of communicating. Having your students write personal letters and then sending them would be special. A couple of years ago Jerry's oldest grandson said it was not fair that his sisters got mail and he did not. He was right; we have lost this special way of communicating that is personal. Save copies of the letters your students write. Create a bulletin board showing copies of the students' letters and the responses they received. In some cases companies send brochures and literature that really enhance the bulletin board.

Emailing

Once you have made a connection with another class it is a good idea to maintain and build on the relationship formed to collaborate on other projects. One way to continue the connection is by using email. In 1999–2000, Jerry participated in an Email Around the World project. It was a fantastic way to connect with students all across the globe. It was long before the ability existed to connect in person via Skype or Google Hangouts or other such tools. Jerry made a great bulletin board, which had a map of the world with the email responses showing where the connections originated. The actual email was connected by yarn to the country on the map where it originated. To see all of the emails that Jerry's classes received in their 1999 Email Around the World project, visit www.angelfire.com/stars3/education/emailworld.html.

Today with the available technology we can easily connect our students almost instantaneously to classrooms around the world. We believe all classroom teachers should flatten the walls of their classroom to communicate, collaborate, and create with other classrooms around the globe and experts in the different fields the students are studying about. Using the myriad of web tools accessible to them, teachers should be reaching out as often as possible to help their students build and strengthen their global connections and add to their personal learning networks.

We feel that it is extremely important when working with your students to connect with them at first and show them that you really care. You should follow this natural progression of teaching connections, starting small and building up to bigger connections. After teacher-to-student relationships are solidified, it is important that students connect with their peers in the classroom and build a sharing, caring community.

A very important first step is working with your students toward being a good citizen in our digital world. We cannot stress enough the importance of **digital citizenship**. Please periodically review with your students how to be responsible users of technology. Explain the need to be careful about what they post online. Children have to be conscious of their digital presence and the **digital footprint** that they are creating. Talk to them about proper **netiquette** when they are connecting online. Please also communicate with their parents and make sure they understand the importance of parents keeping track of what their children are doing online.

The next step is to connect your class with other grade levels and experts outside the classroom. Students should be able to get answers to their questions from experts. You can then connect your students with other classes around the country and the world to learn and share with one another. The initial connections can lead to future collaborations.

The question always asked is, "How do I connect my students to other classes around the country or the world?" This is a major concern among all grade levels. There are many different **social media** venues in which we can connect in today's world—Twitter, **Google+**, **Edmodo**, and **Voxer**, just to name a few. There are groups available for any grade and any subject. Connected Classrooms Workshop on Google+[1] is a great resource for all educators. This community, created by Google for Education with over 15,000 educators, is a wonderful place to start as you can filter by grade level and subject area. You can post to the appropriate grade level or subject area you are teaching and search through the community for specific resources. When you are looking to connect on a project, be sure to ask everyone in the community if they are interested in participating in your project. Google+ communities are an easy way to get started becoming a connected educator.

Another good way to connect is to join communities on Edmodo.[2] We recommend that you sign up for a free Edmodo account to take advantage of all it has to offer. Communities on Edmodo contain the main subject areas of language arts, math, science, and social studies, along with other communities including creative art, health and physical education, and special education. Similar to the communities on Google+, you can post or filter through these communities to find information or other educators to connect with around the world.

Twitter is another great way in which to connect with educators from across the world, and we have found it to be one of the best ways to become a connected educator. Billy, Jerry, and Paula have connected through Twitter and have been able to find many projects to do in their classrooms thanks to this resource. There are chats for most subject areas and grade levels. The schedule for **Twitter educational chats** can be found at bit.ly/educhatcalendar. The weekly chats have provided ideas for both Billy and Paula to bring into their classroom. We have found this to be an easy way to connect with other educators or find a partner to do a project with. It is just a matter of using the appropriate **hashtag (#)** in order to find someone.

What is a hashtag? It is Twitter's way of aggregating tweets about a common topic into searchable data. For example, if you were looking for information about the Daily Five and teaching fourth grade you can tweet: "Looking for information on the #DailyFive **#4thchat**." Anyone who follows those hashtags will see the tweet come across on their timeline and could either respond to it or retweet it to others who might have a better knowledge of the subject. Another example would be if you were a middle school teacher teaching English and were about to start a study group on *The Hunger Games*; you might tweet, "Starting a book study on The Hunger Games. Anyone have any information? #mschat #engchat #edchat."

We have found that an easy entry point to making connections at the elementary level is through Mystery Location Calls using **Skype** or **Google Hangouts**. In Chapter 2, we will explain in depth how to get started with Mystery Location Calls. Participating in a Mystery Location Call is an engaging and tech-infused way to have students practice their geography and communication skills. During the calls students are learning about other parts of the country or world through either inquiry or yes-or-no questions. Mystery Locations Calls are fun and easy to run in your classroom. This book will examine ways in which to conduct a Mystery Location Call and explain the various jobs students have while conducting these calls. We will walk you step by step through the ins and outs of conducting a Mystery Location Call, starting with dividing your class into two groups to practice performing an actual Mystery Location Call. The step-by-step guide will give you the strategies that work best in the classroom.

What else is possible besides Mystery Location Calls? What can you do at different grade levels? We have discussed this point with our weekly Sunday Night Google Hangout group, which consists of teachers from seven different states who have done these calls with their classes. This book could not have been possible without the connections the authors have made with these wonderful educators. We have been working together over the last several years to come up with projects and activities to do as a follow-up to a Mystery Location Call or as an alternative to Mystery Location Calls. Through our connections on Twitter, Facebook, and Google+ and our own creativity, we have compiled a list of projects that teachers can move on to after they have begun collaborations through Mystery Location Calls.

These projects range from short, 20-minute activities to ones that can take place over several weeks. The chapters include other **videoconferencing** ideas. We have provided suggested ways you can collaborate for all the seasons of the year. We have included a chart listing of all the projects (see Table 1.1). It is our hope that this book serves as a guide for ways to get involved with collaborative projects.

Table 1.1 Chapter previews

Chapter 3: Moving Beyond Mystery Location Calls
The projects that we have participated in are denoted by an asterisk (*).

Sharing a Guest Speaker: Veterinarian Live*
Sharing a Guest Speaker: Celebrating the Constitution*
The Winter Olympics
Olympic Game Show Quiz*
Math Competition
Science Fair Challenge
Dry Ice Experiment*
Scientists Help Science Teachers Using Social Media
Flat Stanley and Travel Buddies
Foster Grandparent Program
E-Book
Dreamwakers*

Chapter 4: Fall Projects

September	October
Labor Day	Global Read Aloud (GRA)*
O.R.E.O. Project*	How Weather Affects Us*
September 11: Showing Compassion	Pumpkin Seed Project*
Hispanic Heritage (September 15–October 15)	Halloween Projects
International Dot Day* (September 15)	

November
Election Day
Veterans Day/Remembrance Day
Gettysburg Address*
Native American Heritage Month
Thanksgiving Day: Canada (October) vs. the United States (November)
Plimoth Plantation*

Chapter 5: Winter Projects
*100th Day of School**

December	January
Holiday Card Exchange*	New Year's
RACK—Random Acts of Christmas	Dr. Martin Luther King Jr.*
Kindness*	Martin's Big Words*
Pearl Harbor Day	
12.12.12 Blogging Challenge*	

Chapter 5: Winter Projects
100th Day of School*

February	March
American Heart Month*	Mardi Gras*
Black History Month*	Read Across America—Dr. Seuss's
Groundhog Day	Birthday*
Super Bowl Connections*	Commonwealth Day
Presidents' Day	Pi Day—March 14 (3/14)
Snow Days	St. Patrick's Day*
	Women's History Month

Chapter 6: Spring and Summer Projects

April
National Autism Awareness Month
Standardized Testing*
PictureIt Project*
Impromptu Calls*
Poetry Month*
April Fools' Day
Baseball
Holocaust Remembrance Day
Earth Day—Grocery Bag Project*
Arbor Day

May	June
National Inventors Month	Flag Day
10-Day Passion Challenge and Identity Day*	Graduation—End of School
Cinco de Mayo*	
Memorial Day	

The Next Chapter

In Chapter 2 we will take you through a step-by-step guide for participating in your own Mystery Location Call with your class.

Notes

1. https://plus.google.com/u/0/communities/100662407427957932931.
2. www.edmodo.com/about.

2

The Practical Guide to a
Mystery Location Call

What is a Mystery Location Call? Imagine a classroom activity taking place where many Common Core State Standards from all subject areas and the ISTE Standards (formerly known as the **NETS**) are being addressed all at once (see Appendix A for more information on the ISTE Standards). Now imagine that this same activity addresses the twenty-first-century skills known as the **Four Cs (4Cs)**—collaboration, communication, creativity, and critical thinking. On top of that, this learning adventure is so much fun and so engaging to your students that they will be begging for more.

A Mystery Location Call is an exciting, engaging educational guessing game played by two or more classes. The classes connect using a videoconferencing platform such as Skype or Google Hangouts to figure out where the other class or classes are located. If this is not done with a predetermined game plan, it could take quite a long time. From others who pioneered these calls and through our own experiences we have learned a great deal about how to make these calls very successful and captivating experiences for all the students involved. We are going to take you through those steps so that you too can use Mystery Location Calls to start connecting your students with others. We have also discovered that starting with Mystery Location Calls as your first foray into connecting leads to future collaborations with the teachers and classrooms you meet during your calls.

Mystery Location Calls Subsections

Common Core and ISTE Standards
Inner Workings of a Mystery Location Call
Preparing Students for Mystery Location Calls
Supplies for a Mystery Location Call
Finding People for a Call
Overcoming Different Time Zones to Connect with the World
Jobs for Students
Skills Developed by Students Participating in Mystery Location
    Calls
Sample Inquiry-Based Questions
Sample Yes-or-No Questions
Practicing a Mystery Location Call
After the Call—Making It a Learning Experience
Writing a Blog
What to Do After the First Mystery Location Call to Keep the
    Connections Continuing

(Common Core Standards: RI.6, RL.1, RF, SL) (Post Call: W.1, W.2, W.3, W.7) (Mathematics: MD.1) (ISTE Standards for Students: 2, 3, 5, 6) (ISTE Standards for Teachers: 1, 2, 3, 4)

Inner Workings of a Mystery Location Call

There are some very important parts of the Mystery Location Call that have to take place to ensure a successful connection. Communication with the other teacher(s) is crucial. All involved teachers have to know how the call will work. Running a test of the conferencing tool (Skype, Google Hangouts, etc.) is important. Check the visual and audio parts and see if they are working well. Make sure everyone knows about the time constraints as a typical call lasts about 20 minutes. Discuss the type of questions that the students will prepare. There are typically two different types of questions that people like to use: yes-or-no questions, which are Paula's preference, and inquiry-based questions, which are Billy's preference. Examples of both of these types of questions appear later in this chapter.

Occasionally students will quickly be able to discover the state where the other class is located. To keep the call going, you could have the class try to also figure out the city where the other class is located. The students have to really think and become great researchers in order to correctly guess the city, but it does work and it is fun to watch students in this challenge. We will provide sample questions to help guide you through this part as well.

Preparing Students for Mystery Location Calls

The teacher needs to explain how a Mystery Location Call works. We suggest watching some **YouTube** videos of other classes that have participated in these calls. While watching these videos, students should keep track of what they liked and did not like, as well as ideas about how to improve those calls. To motivate your students, show them the Super Bowl ad for Microsoft featuring an Irvine, California, classroom doing a Mystery Location Call.[1] Have your students practice communication skills with and without technology—listening, speaking (enunciating, pace, tone, volume)—and be aware of **body language**, including eye contact and **microexpressions**. Have your students view the video of the practice call so they can watch and listen to themselves to find ways they can improve their body language and speech.

The teacher might want to set up a reminder using the **Remind** app to keep the students and parents up to date on the upcoming Mystery Location Call and what needs to be done.

Before the actual call, it is necessary to have your students do research on their state and city and start coming up with clues to be used during the call. You can group the clues into easy, medium, or hard. Have the class vote on which clues to use.

Before starting any Mystery Location Call, Billy has his students complete a project, usually a **PowerPoint** or other computer project, on New Jersey and their city. The goal is that the students have prior knowledge about the state and city before doing Mystery Location Calls that involve inquiry-based questions. The students should be able to answer questions similar to those that will be used during a call. Some of the questions are as follows:

In what region of the United States is our state located?
What is the capital of our state?
Name two rivers that flow through our state.

Name three famous people from our state and tell why they are
   famous.
What are some products that our state is known for?
List two to four famous landmarks found in our state.
What is our state flower?
What is our state bird?
In what time zone are we located?
What kind of animals do we find in our state?
Name two states that border our state.

Supplies for a Mystery Location Call

Before starting a Mystery Location Call it is important to have certain supplies available in order to help make the call easier. The following supplies
are recommended: a computer that connects to the Internet with a **webcam**
(this is a necessity), microphones, maps of the United States or the world,
pencils, erasers, scrap paper, computers for students, clipboards, photo
camera, video camera, and clocks showing different times zones. There are
many sources from which to obtain free or inexpensive supplies and equipment for your class, including these major sources: DonorsChoose, Digital
Wish, Adopt a Classroom, and ClassWish. We highly recommend letting
your parent-teacher organization, parents of your students, and businesses
in your community know about your needs. You can also write a grant to
obtain the items you need.

   Billy uses the following setup when he does his calls: a Yeti Microphone and a Microsoft Lifecam on a tripod, which works great, and a USB
extender. (Please note that the webcam he uses is not compatible with an
Apple computer.)

Finding People for a Call

There are many ways that you can find teachers willing to do a Mystery
Location Call with your class. Social media has made it much easier to find
other classes with which to conduct Mystery Location Calls and other collaborative activities. Twitter has flattened the world and provided a great
way to connect with teachers all over the world. Different grade-specific
Twitter Chats have produced lists of teachers willing to do Mystery Location Calls.

Overcoming Different Time Zones to Connect with the World

In order to connect classes from all over the globe, it is necessary to be creative. You may have to pre-record sessions and questions. If you cannot connect because of time zone issues, have your students come up with a Mystery Location Scavenger Hunt for the other class to use to find your location. Open school evenings or family event nights also provide chances to connect. Enlist the school librarian to help carry out these connections with students attending the parent-teacher evening sessions.

There are two convenient ways to connect with other classrooms in various time zones. The first is on Google+, where a community called "Mystery Location Calls" is established. The second, Skype in the Classroom, has a #MysterySkype page where you can find contacts by location and age group.[2]

Jobs for Students

To have a successful and engaging experience, each student in the class should have a function during a Mystery Location Call. Practicing will ensure a successful call. Divide the class into two groups and go through a trial call in class without using a connecting tool. Please film this practice call so that the entire class can review it to see how they functioned. Have each group secretly pick a different state than the one they live in. Make sure the students know exactly what their jobs entail. Tell the students that during future calls the jobs will be rotated. Also keep in mind our jobs list is a suggestion. Feel free to add to or subtract from this list as needed. Just remember that for the most successful experience during Mystery Location Calls, each student needs to be actively engaged.

The following is a description of jobs that you can employ with your students. Select the ones that you and your students are most comfortable with using. Depending on your class size and their feelings, adjust the number of students for the jobs that you have selected. There is a lot of flexibility in the different jobs, allowing for classes of different sizes to adjust to meet the need of their classes.

Lead Student: The Lead Student is like the director of a movie who makes sure everything runs smoothly and jobs are being done well. This job entails troubleshooting problems that arise, keeping the call moving, and in dead spots inserting Entertainers to keep the call interesting. Have this student draw a diagram of the classroom and the location of all the jobs. The Lead Student can decide how many students are needed for each job and can install an assistant to help. Directly after the call the Lead Student should start a Google Document on things that need improvement. The Lead Student should then have the other students in the class add to the document. We suggest that one student handle this very important job.

Visual Arts Director: This job is equivalent to the person in charge of the scenery and props used on a movie set. This student should carefully watch a film of the classroom during the trial call to make the part of the classroom that will be seen on the video call looks good and does not give any clues to the actual location. The Visual Arts Director makes sure that there are necessary visual aids for the call. They have to ensure that there are signs for the class and name cards (only use given names) for Greeters, Questioners, and Answerers. We suggest one student handle this job.

Greeter: The Greeter is like the emcee: this person welcomes the other class in a fun way without revealing their location. This student needs excellent verbal and nonverbal communication skills. Sometimes this person can also end the call. This function can be combined with the Closer job. It is wise to have a name card with the student's given name only and have a banner of the class in the background. We suggest having one to two students for this job.

Question Developers (Researchers): The Question Developers are like scriptwriters. They design clever questions and provide the questions and their answers to the Question Reviewers. It is important that the teachers in the call discuss the type of questions (most calls use only yes-or-no questions) to be used during the call to make sure there is no confusion among the students. Students can develop a database of questions in different categories to assist in development of appropriate questions. Arrange this group near the Question Reviewers and Questioners. This job could have a number of students, anywhere from two to six depending on the size of the class.

Question Reviewers: They decide on the order of these questions. These students must listen closely to the interchange. They analyze the questions and answers from the Question Developers to make sure they follow what has taken place so far during the call. They have to be prepared to change the next question(s) as a result of what they hear. They can employ Runners, who take questions to the Questioner or, if allowed, text the question. Given that the previous job could have a number of students, we would suggest that this job could also have more than one student. Ideally you want to have at least two students doing this job, but you can have anywhere from two to six students depending on the size of the class. The overall idea is to always make sure every student has a job and is doing something during the call.

Questioners: The Questioners have to ask the questions in a clear voice that can be heard and easily understood. We suggest that you have a boy and a girl perform this job. They can alternate asking the questions. If you have a smaller class this job can be combined with the Greeters.

Answerers: These students need to brainstorm and come up with logical answers to the questions they are asked. Students can employ appropriate tech tools (graphic organizers, **spreadsheets**, **databases**, etc.) to help with their predictions and draw conclusions. They need to choose one member of the group to give the answer. We suggest as many as four students could be in this group.

Geographers: The Geographers have to quickly analyze the clues given by the opposing class. Using wall maps, atlases, or maps on computers, they have to narrow down the area to search. They work along with the Map Puzzlers. Place these two teams close to one another. We suggest that there be a few students for each team.

Map Puzzlers or Logical Reasoners: Map Puzzlers or Logical Reasoners remove states, cities, or countries that have been eliminated by clues that have been given. It is a good idea to have a jigsaw puzzle of the United States or the world, depending on the call. If you do not have puzzle maps and are only having Logical Reasoners, allow them to work with the Geographers to figure out where the call is coming from. We recommend three to five students for the job depending on your class size.

Runners: The Runners transfer information between the different jobs during the call. Make sure there is a clear path between the stations. If you have a **BYOD (Bring Your Own Device)** policy in place, you can have "runners" text the information between stations. We suggest between two and four students for this job.

Backchannelers: This job requires that your students have access to devices that are connected to the Internet. A **backchannel** is a digital conversation that happens at the same time as a face-to-face activity. While the Mystery Location Call is happening, students are on devices using web tools like TodaysMeet or an Edmodo group as their backchannel platform. They type what is being said during the Mystery Location Call and chat with students from the other location. It is very important that the backchannelers do not reveal any information while chatting that could give away their location. Determine ahead of time if the other class will have students who will be backchanneling, decide on the platform, and share the address to the TodaysMeet room or the code to the Edmodo group prior to the start of the call. The number of students who are assigned this job will depend on the number of devices you have access to. Four to five students is ideal.

Photographers/Videographers: The camera crew takes still images and a videotape of the call. It is important that schools have parental permission to post any videos or photos of students. Usually, permission for a Mystery Location Call is not needed if it is not being recorded. Double-check with your school's **Acceptable Use Policy** regarding recording and photographing students. There are also programs you can use if you need to blur out a student's face. The number of students for the Photographer/Videographer job depends on how many cameras you have access to and the number of students in the class. Create a multimedia presentation of the call when it is concluded. Make sure you have at least one to two students for this job, though the maximum number of students recommended is four.

Time Keeper: The Time Keeper keeps the Mystery Location Call going within the time limit, which is usually about 20 minutes. This student can utilize a computer countdown timer, watch, or clock and should hold up easily read time signs. The time signs indicating minutes left can be prepared in advance. He or she can also use a bell to indicate one minute left. We recommend only one student for this position.

Tech Help Squad: The student Tech Help Squad will be ready to troubleshoot technology problems to help the teacher make sure the call works. They will ensure that students can be heard and seen. They are responsible for carrying out visual and sound checks before and during the call. The following jobs are part of this team: Sound Engineer, Visual Director, and Tech Troubleshooter. We recommend at least three students.

Social Media Sharers: Decide on a special hashtag (#) for this event and have students report on the progress of the call on Twitter. You can also share pictures and stories on Facebook. Remember: if using social media make sure you eliminate your location on your biography. One student would be perfect for this job. If you have a large class, consider using different types of social media, but it would be tough for multiple students to be using one Twitter account at a time.

Entertainers: To liven up the call during breaks, have students share some jokes or songs. You could have several entertainers during the Mystery Location Call. They need to prepare and rehearse their parts in advance. This can really help enhance the experience of the call. The Lead Student will determine when to insert the Entertainer to keep the call running smoothly and keep everyone interested. We recommend having one or two students available for this job.

Bloggers: These students are taking notes about the Mystery Location Call and will write a **blog** post about the experience. The blog post will be shared with the other classes to promote future connections and collaborations. The ideal number for this job is one or two students. This can also be a great writing experience for a whole class activity.

State Facts Sharers: Once the state or city of the class has been determined, have some students share some interesting facts about their state, city, and school. Some examples of things to share are famous people, interesting sights, products manufactured, or produce the state might be known for. Tell the other class about your school—its mascot, prominent graduates—and some fun facts about your community. We suggest you have these students create a database or spreadsheet of these state facts. If time has run out, please share these facts with the other class by mail, either regular or electronic, or on a blog. This will continue the exchange between the classes.

Closers: The Closers end the call by thanking the other class for their participation in the call. After the location has been determined, the Closers can share interesting products from your state. For example, students in a school in Michigan displayed cereals produced in their state. Have the Closers prepared to open the door to future collaborations by inviting the other class to visit your blog or send emails, or encourage them to have a suggestion of a topic for a future video call. Ideas for a follow-up video call include surveying each other about favorite items and doing a presentation or a demonstration for the other class, which could include singing a song, reciting poetry, doing a science demo, or debating an interesting topic. The page www.cybraryman.com/states.html has a lot of information you can use. Ideally it would be nice to have one or two students as Closers.

These jobs are ones that we have found worked well or that have been successful with others in their classrooms. Keep in mind that the number of students for each job can vary according to your class size. Feel free to find what works best for your class since every classroom setting and environment is different.

Skills Developed by Students Participating in Mystery Location Calls

During these calls, students develop many different skills that are valuable in today's world. Reading and writing standards are addressed through these global projects by having the students work on collaborative **Google Documents**. In preparation for these calls the students perform a myriad of research skills. During the call they use online resources to research clues. Reading and writing skills are also addressed as the students backchannel in either Edmodo or TodaysMeet. They practice communication skills by speaking, listening, and engaging in nonverbal communication while participating in the videoconferencing calls. After the videoconference concludes, the students should blog or write about their experiences. They can also start communicating more with the other class via a safe, closed social learning network like Edmodo.

Teachers should model for their students how to work in our digital age. Teachers make global connections via Twitter, Google+, and other social media sites to enable their students to collaborate with other students around the globe.

A number of these skills fall under the 21st Century Student Outcomes and Support System put out by the Partnership for 21st Century Skills.[3] Students develop and enhance their critical thinking and problem solving skills during Mystery Location Calls. Students need to think quickly and use reasoning skills to answer the questions they are being asked. Since these calls are live, students also need to be able to use deductive reasoning skills at a moment's notice to solve the puzzle of where in the world the other class is located.

You may not at first think that creativity fits the concept of Mystery Location Calls; however, students are coming up with questions as well as asking them. They are brainstorming on their feet and being creative in how they ask questions along with the ways in which they are solving the location.

Today it is important for students to learn how to collaborate with one another. During Mystery Location Calls, teamwork skills are enhanced as the students work together to solve a mystery and solve problems. Students communicate and collaborate with a global audience via Skype or Google Hangouts as they participate in Mystery Location Calls. This leads to classrooms collaborating on other projects. They learn and model proper digital citizenship and communication skills as they ask and answer the clues that help them discover where the other class is located. One of the major 21st Century Skills that a Mystery Location Call addresses is **collaboration**. Students collaborate and learn team building both with their classmates and with students outside of their classroom.

Another valuable skill used in these calls is time management. Since there is usually a limited amount of time for each call, the students have to use it wisely. Decision making not only goes along with time management but is also an important skill for students to learn early on. Students need to know how to make quick decisions and eliminate states in which the other class is not located. This leads us to another skill learned during a Mystery Location Call: **deductive reasoning**. Students have to deduce which states can be eliminated based on the information uncovered through each answered question.

Students are becoming globally aware of their surroundings. During Mystery Location Calls we are breaking down the walls of our classroom and showing students the world around them. It is important in today's world for students to become globally aware of other cultures and how we all look different but can become connected. Other proficiencies being taught are geography skills and research skills, both of which are very important to any learner and should be taught at all age levels.

Looking at all of the skills we come to realize how important it is to be digitally literate. We must make sure we are talking to students about **digital literacy** and how we are using digital skills during these calls. You should also be talking about the importance of being a good digital citizen.

Sample Inquiry-Based Questions

How would you describe the weather now?

Do you experience any extreme weather? If so, what kind?

Do you live in an urban, suburban, or rural area?

What time is it where you are right now? (This is a great question for students to gain an understanding of other time zones around the world.)

What kind of agriculture products are grown in your state?

What are some animals that you might see in the wild in your state?

What are some famous places, tourist attractions, or popular events from your state?

Who are some of the famous people born in your state?

What is your state's nickname?

Does your state border any bodies of water? If so, please name it.

What region of the United States are you located in?

Name one state that borders your state.

What is your state's capital?

Once the students guess the state, if there is enough time left, have them try to determine the city the other class is located in. If you decide to end with just the state location, make sure you are prepared to share some information about your state and even your school and classroom.

What is the name of your school?
  a. Where is your school located?
  b. How many students are in your school?
  c. What grades does your school include?
  d. Does your school have a mascot or motto?
  e. Briefly describe some things that you like about your school.
  f. What language do kids in your classroom speak other than English? What other languages are children fluent in?

Sample Yes-or-No Questions

Are you in the United States?
Are you (east/west) of the Mississippi River?
Are you in the (Eastern, Central, Mountain, Pacific, etc.) time zone?
Is your state in the (Northeast, Southeast, Southwest, Midwest, or West) region?
Does your state border (Canada/Mexico)?
Does your state border more than ___ states?
Does your state have a coastline?
Does your state border the (Atlantic/Pacific) Ocean or Gulf of Mexico?
Is your state east of the Rocky Mountains?
Does the ____ River flow through your state?
Does your state's name have two words in it?
Does the name of your state have a Native American origin?
Does your state/country start with the letter ___?
Is there a major river that borders your state?
Is your state landlocked?

Practicing a Mystery Location Call

As we have stated before in the section "Jobs for Students," we suggest carrying out a practice call. Divide the class in half and have them select students for all the jobs. Let them decide on their mystery locations. Videotape the practice and go over with the entire class the good points and those that need to be improved. You could also try the call with another class in your school to make sure everything will run smoothly.

During the practice session have the photographers take pictures. Check the audio of your equipment and the students. The teacher should definitely connect with the other teacher on a Skype or Google Hangouts call to make sure the connection works and the audio is fine. Make students aware that they should not give away clues to their location. On the Mystery Location Call day do not wear any clothes that indicate your location; for example, clothing featuring professional sports teams usually show those from your state or city. Make sure students know the time period of the call. You need to keep within that time frame, so questions and answers have to be timed. Plan the time schedule with the other teacher beforehand.

After the Call—Making It a Learning Experience

So was this activity a learning experience? To find out, have each student complete an **exit slip** recording what they learned during the Mystery Location Call. This is a great formative assessment of their learning. They can include what worked and what did not work so you can make adjustments for your future Mystery Location Calls. Believe us when we say that your students will be begging for more of them.

Writing a Blog

Writing a blog is a great way to have your students discuss their experience participating in a Mystery Location Call. Share the students' blog posts with the class they connected with and have them respond and comment. The blog posts can be shared with other classes as well. The use of the hashtag #comments4kids, created by William Chamberlain (@wmchamberlain), enables the children to get comments from people outside the walls of their classroom. Blogging gives even the quietest student a global voice.

Figure 2.1

3	Things I Learned Today . . .
2	Things I Found Interesting . . .
1	Question I Still Have . . .

What to Do after the First Mystery Location Call to Continue the Connections

Before you end your first Mystery Location Call, set a date and time to reconnect with this class. Before the next video call, each class will have the students create a series of survey questions that can be asked of the other class during the call. Have the classes take turns interviewing each other and gathering the answers to the survey questions. As your second call with this class is wrapping up, set another date and time to connect; each class then turns the previously collected data into graphs before sharing how your class's answers compare to their class's answers. Now one Mystery Location Call has been turned into three collaborative connections with the same group of students.

Resources

There are many different resources out there for Mystery Location Calls or Mystery Skype Calls. Here are a few that we found useful.

Four Cs: www.cybraryman.com/4cs.html

Geography: www.cybraryman.com/geography.html

Google Hangouts: www.cybraryman.com/googlehangout.html

Mrs. Carroll's Classroom Blog: Mystery State Skype Preparation: www.mrscarroll310. blogspot.com/2012/09/mystery-state-skype-preparation.html

ITM42, Mystery Location Calls video on YouTube: www.youtube.com/watch?v= q0dpOXXMBMg

Ms. Naugle's Classroom Blog: Our First Mystery Location Call Using Google Hangout: www.pnaugle.blogspot.com/2012/10/our-first-mystery-state-google-hangout.html

Mystery Location Call: www.cybraryman.com/mysterylocationcall.html

Mystery Location Call Resources page—Billy Krakower: http://www.billykrakower. com/mystery-location-call-resources-page.html

Powell4thGrade: Our Very First Mystery Skype This Year with Our New Friends in Ohio! www.powell4thgrade.blogspot.com/2011/10/our-very-first-mystery-skype-this-year.html

Regruth Hub: Our First Mystery Skype! www.brownroom18.blogspot.com/2013/08/our-first-mystery-skype.html

Remind: www.cybraryman.com/remind.html
Skype: www.cybraryman.com/skype.html
Skype in the Classroom: https://education.skype.com

The Next Chapter

Now that you have an understanding of the Mystery Location Call, in Chapter 3 we will share other ways you can connect and collaborate. We are going to present ideas to connect classes during the course of the school year in the forthcoming chapters.

Notes

1. *Mystery Skype: Connecting Classrooms Around the World*, www.youtube.com/watch?v=GZdMnkWHG7s.
2. https://education.skype.com.
3. www.p21.org/our-work/p21-framework.

3

Moving Beyond Mystery Location Calls

After the initial Mystery Location Call where you have established a relationship with the other class, there are a myriad of ways you can take it further. In this chapter we will discuss different ideas on how to connect and enhance the learning of your students.

Inviting a guest speaker to visit your classroom is a wonderful way to bring the community into your school. You can take that experience to the next level by sharing the guest speaker with other classes via videoconferencing. Share your best lesson, science demonstration, or tech tip with other classes by becoming a "guest teacher."

When Billy brought in a veterinarian to talk with his students, he was able to connect with several classrooms across the United States to share this special learning event. Paula will share her experiences of having Dan Curcio, "Dan, Dan the Science Man" (@dandanscience), videoconference with her class to do science demonstrations. She will also show how she shares her classroom guest speaker, James Adams, an expert on the Constitution and the Bill of Rights, with other classrooms around the country. We will share a story from Dan Curcio about "Scientists Help Science Teachers Using Social Media." Jerry will show how he has connected with classes all around the country and in some other parts of the world.

The technological age has enabled us to share our adventures with the world as they occur.

Chapter 3: Moving Beyond Mystery Location Calls

The projects that we have participated in are denoted by an asterisk (*).

Sharing a Guest Speaker: Veterinarian Live*
Sharing a Guest Speaker: Celebrating the Constitution*
The Winter Olympics
Olympic Game Show Quiz*
Math Competition
Science Fair Challenge
Dry Ice Experiment/Decomposers*
Scientists Help Science Teachers Using Social Media
Flat Stanley and Travel Buddies
Foster Grandparent Program
E-Book
Dreamwakers*

Sharing a Guest Speaker: Veterinarian Live*

(Common Core State Standards: SL) (ISTE Standards for Students: 2, 5)
(ISTE Standards for Teachers: 1, 2, 3, 4)

It is important that we provide our students with opportunities to learn about different careers to help them prepare for their future. For the past several years, Billy has brought in to his classroom Dr. Mark Salemi of Northside Animal Hospital (www.nahnyc.com), a veterinarian who works in the community. The veterinarian discussed what he does for a living. He also brought with him several animals and explained how he treated them. What made these visits so special was that Billy shared this experience with other classrooms around the country using a Google Hangout. It was a great, engaging, and fun learning opportunity for everyone involved.

Bringing in a community member in person or by using technology tools like Skype or Google Hangouts is an easy way to start connecting beyond the walls of your classroom. Dr. Salemi is also a Board of Education member and wanted to give back to the school community. We highly recommend that you survey your students' parents and find out if they would be willing to share about their careers. This can be accomplished by a classroom visit in person, a visit to their work site, or a Skype call or Google Hangout. Share this learning experience with other classes

Figure 3.1 Dr. Salemi showing students in New Jersey, New Orleans, and Massachusetts a Turtle shell.

Figure 3.2 Dr. Salemi showing a ferret to the students both in the room and virtually.

in other schools by connecting them as well. All you need is an Internet connection, a webcam, and a microphone. We suggest that you save these wonderful learning events and build a library to share with students who were absent, future classes, or other classes in your school or in other schools.

Dr. Salemi observes, "Connecting with children by speaking to and interacting with them in a classroom setting is always a great thrill. Talking to them about what I love to do every day and seeing how they become so engaged makes it a great experience. The ability of being able to speak to children in three states at one time through technology, now available to the schools, is a wonderful way for the children to learn and interact with other school districts. Most of all, the smiles and enthusiasm experienced during these video calls make these sessions very memorable."

Sharing a Guest Speaker: Celebrating the Constitution*

(Common Core State Standards: SL) (Social Studies Standards: refer to your state standards or curriculum) (ISTE Standards for Students: 2, 5) (ISTE Standards for Teachers: 1, 2, 3, 4)

Paula has a good friend, James Adams, who is an expert on the Constitution and the Bill of Rights. Her fourth graders need to have a basic understanding of both of these as part of their social studies curriculum. She has invited James into her classroom for the last several years to share his expertise with her students. One day when James showed up, he was surprised to see another class projected on the **interactive whiteboard** in Paula's classroom. Paula explained that he would be sharing not only with her class but also with another class in Kansas. A webcam was set up so that he could be seen and heard by the other class. Needless to say, James was a little surprised by the technical setup, but as he gave his presentation he was amazed at the collaboration taking place. Not only could Paula's students ask and answer questions, but so could Jan Wells's (@janwells) class in Kansas. Both of these fourth-grade classrooms had students on computers logged into an Edmodo collaborative group, backchanneling about the information that James was presenting. Now that Paula uses Google Hangouts, James has been able to do his presentation for several classes in different locations at the same time.[1]

The Olympics

(Common Core State Standards: SL) (ISTE Standards for Students: 2, 3, 5)
(ISTE Standards for Teachers: 1, 2, 3, 4)

The Olympic Games garner a lot of attention every two years, alternating between Summer and Winter games. Students are excited about the Olympics Games, therefore it becomes an engaging way to get students excited about learning. The Olympic games allow us to be able to teach many different subject areas at once. We can discuss geography, mathematics, and science all in one lesson while getting students excited about the subject. This is also relevant to what is going on in the world around us. Today, we are even able to connect with each other about the Olympics and with athletes in the Olympic Village.

Several members of #4thchat were lucky enough to be able to connect during the 2014 Winter Olympics and had a friendly little competition with our classrooms doing an Olympic Game Show. Another great way of exposing students to the sporting and cultural events is to videoconference with the Olympic Village. Jennifer Regruth was able to connect her classroom and shares her experience with the historic event and even how she obtained this exciting opportunity.

Videoconferencing with the Olympic Village

(Common Core State Standards: SL) (ISTE Standards for Students: 2, 3, 5)
(ISTE Standards for Teachers: 1, 2, 3, 4)

During the Olympics, Jennifer Regruth's classroom was able to connect with a gold medal winner in bobsledding live from the athlete village in Sochi, Russia! Several classes joined together in a Google Hangout (GHO) for this historic live video chat. With classes from Pennsylvania, California, Oregon, Michigan, Indiana and New York, we got to hear first hand about the village for the athletes, competition, food in the cafeteria, and what an honor it is to compete for the USA. One of the kids even asked if the athletes played tricks on each other!

A few days later, the classes watched live as Meryl Davis and Charlie White won their gold medals in ice dancing! We were so proud! Then in early May, Jennifer's class had our 2nd live chat with them! We made signs and chanted, "USA!" Then they showed us their gold medals and we were able to ask questions about their experience. Using technology to connect "face to face" and in groups is a game changer.

Olympic Game Show Quiz

(Common Core State Standards: RI, W, SL) (ISTE Standards for Students: 2, 3, 4) (ISTE Standards for Teachers: 1, 2, 3, 4)

During the 2014 Winter Olympics, Billy (in New Jersey), Paula (in Louisiana), Nancy (in Massachusetts), and Jennifer (in Indiana) used Google Hangouts for their classrooms to have a little competition about the Olympic Games. Before the competition the students did a lot of research and were well prepared with some very well-thought-out and challenging questions. We gave each class a special sound effect so we were able to easily determine which class responded first to a question. Jerry (in Florida) hosted and moderated this spirited game show.

Some of the questions used were these:

When were the first Winter Olympic Games?
Name four Winter Olympic sports.
Where does the flame for the Olympic torch originate?
What medals are awarded to Olympic champions?
Where are the Olympics being held?
What four Winter Olympic competitions are held indoors?
What country has won the most Winter Olympic gold medals?

Our weekly Google Hangout on Sunday evenings consists of teachers in seven different states, giving us the opportunity to talk about different projects we can do with our students and how to connect our classes. We are always looking for ways to keep up with what is happening in the world or how to celebrate events. When the Olympic Games were approaching, we thought using the events as inspiration would be a fun way to connect our classes.

Math Competition

(Common Core State Standards: SL, OA, MD, NBT, MD, G) (ISTE Standards for Students: 2, 3, 4) (ISTE Standards for Teachers: 1, 2, 3, 4)

Plan a live math competition (similar to the Olympic Game Show) among classes via a Google Hangout or Skype session. Determine the math level of each class and what they have studied. The emcee or moderator of the challenge will ask the questions, and the first team to respond will be given the chance to answer the question. The questions can be developed by a class on the same level who is not participating (but will be observing and ready to alter the questions) in the competition. Assign a special sound effect for each class to use so it will be easier to determine who was first to answer. Award gold, silver, and bronze medal certificates based on points earned to the top three classes. Prior to the competition, have students in the classes that will be participating design award certificates using technology tools. You can have a contest between classes before the actual competition to pick the most creative and technologically savvy certificates.

Science Fair Challenge

(Many different Common Core State Standards and Next Generation Science Standards could fit here depending upon the Science Fair Challenge. Here are a few suggested ones.)
(Common Core State Standards: W.6, W.7, W.8, W.9, MD, G) (Next Generation Science Standards: PS, LS, ESS) (ISTE Standards for Students: 2, 3, 5, 6) (ISTE Standards for Teachers: 1, 2, 3)

Each year students are usually required to do a science fair project. We suggest using this as way for students from different classes to share their science projects. Put your students' projects online so that they can be seen by students in the connecting class. Have the other class's students test out the projects and then send their feedback. The data collected could be added to the original project idea. This could also be an opportunity to come up with a collaborative science fair project on which two or more classes work together. A third class could be used to judge the projects from both classes and come up with ribbons or badges for the projects they feel earned first, second, or third place.

Dry Ice Experiment/Decomposers*

(Common Core State Standards: SL) (Next Generation Science Standards: PS1A, PS1B) (ISTE Standards for Students: 2, 3, 5, 6) (ISTE Standards for Teachers: 1, 2, 3)

When Paula was a "new to science" teacher, she was managing to cover the grade-level expectations for her fourth-grade science curriculum, but she felt ill-equipped to do many demonstrations or experiments with her students. Enter Dan Curcio, "Dan, Dan the Science Man," one of her PLN members from New Jersey. During one of the Sunday Night Google Hangouts that Paula and Dan participate in most weeks, Dan mentioned that he was doing a dry ice demonstration with his students the following week. Paula asked him if it would be possible for her fourth graders to be part of his science class virtually. They agreed to do a Google Hangout so that Dan could share his dry ice demos with her students. At the designated time, they connected via GHO and watched as Dan did some incredible things with dry ice.

As a result of the success of this first virtual science class run by Dan, both classes connected again a few weeks later. This time he led a lively discussion about producers, consumers, and decomposers. Then Dan introduced Curly, Larry, and Mo—his class centipedes—to Paula's students. All of the students loved seeing these creatures up close, even though they were in New Jersey.

These are examples of the wonderful learning opportunities that can happen when you connect your students to others beyond your classroom.

Story from a Member of Our PLN

Dan Curcio Story: Scientists Help Science Teachers Using Social Media

Following is a story from one of the members of the Sunday Night Google Hangout, Dan Curcio (@dandanscience) from New Jersey. He discusses in a blog post how scientists help science teachers using social media. Dan is a passionate science educator at the Community School in Teaneck, New

Jersey. He has shared amazing projects with us and has even allowed some classes to observe and participate using either Skype or Google Hangouts during different experiments.

> Making connections with many individuals *"in the field"* of education over Twitter has enhanced my professional development tenfold. I continue to learn from so many varying perspectives and then can reflect on what I am doing. It has helped bring some wonderful tools into my classroom as I follow the journey of others. I also have begun to follow some great scientists, science graduate students and science writers that are actually *"in the field"* of science. Not all, but many of their posts have been informative and inspiring. A lot of their posts reflect the passion they have for their field of study which I must say has been contagious. I see how passionate some of these professionals can be in wanting to change and benefit this world. It immediately inspires me to get into my classroom and try to spread that passion to my students. We as science teachers can be the bridge between the possible passion in the field to the possible passion in the class. It is our job to inspire our students into being part of the change in the world and not just watching it from afar. Unfortunately, passion can be dulled in a learning environment for students. It seems to be our job to not allow this but instead to IGNITE passion with any and all means possible. Even OUR passion for teaching science can get bogged down at times due to many expectations put upon us. Sometimes we just need HELP. This is where I think social media can actually come in handy. (It's not always about what Justin Beiber [*sic*] had for breakfast, but if that is what you want it can be.) We can connect with like-minded or different-minded individuals to help us reflect our way through. For me I have found a couple "rock stars" in the science field that in following have excited me about what I can teach. It started when I began following an amazing Science teacher Adam Taylor @2footgiraffe and his awesome hashtag that connects scientists to students in a weekly chat, #scistuchat. Being involved in a couple of those Twitter chats I have seen some of the wonderful engagement between "field" and "class"! This pushes me to find more of these professionals and somehow connect. Just knowing of the great scientists or science writers to follow on Twitter is a great start for me. Then down the road hopefully they can see the impact they can have on science teachers and more importantly students

and would even be willing to interact with us. This could lead to making authentic connections between the science field and the classroom at any age range!

I must mention two folks in the field that have recently absolutely inspired my science thinking with some exciting tweets. Alex Wild @Myrmecos with wonderful passion and facts about entomology, he confirms my lessons to students to appreciate the beauty, importance and power of what is thought of as "ugly." David Shiffman @WhySharksMatter with his powerful online presence giving the deserved respect to more amazing creatures that have been sensationalized to the point of destruction! His passion for conservation gets me all riled up which opens up great dialogue with students when "Sharknado" and "Jaws 2000 3D" are blaring through culture.

With all this said, I obviously want more of these folks in my Twitter stream as a Science teacher. I know there are many more of them out there and hope they catch wind of how great their influence can be!! So, let us find them!!! I included a form that I hope will lead to a comprehensive list of scientists, researchers, writers, grad students and Science teachers that are willing to use social media and connect with each other. Selfishly, it will be a great list to benefit my enthusiasm but will hopefully spread to the many students I encounter! Please pass this on and share and share some more with all walks of life in the GLOBAL science and teaching community![2]

Takeaways from Dan's Story

Dan's story illustrates the great benefits of being a connected educator, which allows you to keep up with the latest happenings in education, network with and learn from passionate educators and other experts in your field, learn firsthand from scientists, and share lessons or activities. Making these connections with experts outside the classroom via social media will inspire and ignite your students' passion to learn more.

Flat Stanley and Travel Buddies

Flat Stanley and **Travel Buddies** give students an opportunity to learn about other countries and cultures as well as to appreciate their own community and culture more. These projects connect students at first and can lead to collaboration. Flat Stanley was a book written by Jeff Brown, about a boy who was flattened by a Bulletin Board and had many adventures. The book inspired the Flat Stanley Project, in which Flat Stanley gets passed along to other classrooms and locations across the globe. *Students* keep track of the travels of Flat Stanley by writing letters and taking pictures of the Flat Stanleys they send to others. If you get a Flat Stanley and have to do an adventure, we would suggest the following supplies: fishing line (to hang him up), masking tape (to secure him), and a dowel stick.[3]

Meghan Everette's Story: "Making Connections With Flat Stanley: Framed in France"[4]

Here is a story from one of another member of our PLN, Meghan Everette (@bamameghan) in Alabama, that was featured on the Scholastic blog:[5]

Our school took on the challenge of "Going Global" this year. Each grade is identified by a continent, and in our second year of 1:1, we are reading, learning, and connecting with places all over the globe. It's an exciting time to be in school, but often, young students aren't familiar with geography and have a hard time understanding distances as well as the cultures of places far away. Welcome familiar face Flat Stanley who helped us explore the world from our classroom!

We started the year reading *Flat Stanley* following a simple lesson plan. [See Appendix 3A for lesson plan.] Last year, my students made "reading buddies" out of the Stanley template to have around the room. This year we actually put Stanley *in the mail*! Our "class Stanley" is traveling from city to city, with his adventures being recorded on a digital form. The form is linked to a Google Map so all the first grade classes can log in and see where he has gone.

The next part of the lesson plan involves the kids individually mailing off "Stanleys." Here's what we do:

- ◆ Parents send in addresses of far away family or friends.
- ◆ Parents donate postage stamps (so I don't have to buy them).
- ◆ We make a paper Stanley and mail him with a letter.
- ◆ The letter asks for them to have an "adventure" with Stanley, take photos, and send Stanley back.
- ◆ The stuff we have gotten back has been great. (Grandparents have been *wonderful* about sending elaborate packages back!)

Figure 3.3 Flat Stanley and pictures from around the world.

My class loves Stanley. I cut a full-size boy from insulation sheeting with a heat knife. Stanley swung from the ceiling like a kite, but has now joined our class. Kids walk by and give him high-fives each day and say hello. I decided we needed to keep reading, and selected the latest Stanley story, *Framed in France*, as our next class book. Though not all my first graders are at the level where they can read the story, I have a class set to encourage them to follow along and give them a sense of autonomy over reading a chapter book. They love being able to see the pictures firsthand.

While reading, we created a scrapbook of our time in France with Stanley. Our books are simply four folded pages with a cardstock

Figure 3.4 Flat Stanley and pictures from around the world.

cover. Students folded the books. I downloaded and printed pictures and pieces we would need. Everyone was able to decorate the cover of their scrapbook with stickers and travel items. Then we added information to our book as we read each chapter. It's hard to say what they looked forward to more: reading or scrapbooking! . . .

My students were excited and talking. I heard about plans to buy and read more Stanley adventures from the upcoming book fair. They impressed the art teacher with their knowledge of famous French artists and they have been bringing in sketches and funny versions of the *Mona Lisa*. Stanley helped make a connection to a memorable character, series of books, art, and the world through one simple and fun-to-read story.

Takeaways from Meghan's Story

Starting with something familiar and expanding it into a collaborative project is an easy way to start making global connections. Try to get your whole school involved by having each grade level participate. Reach out to the students' families (especially grandparents) to help with your project.

Besides extending the reading and writing curriculum, brainstorm how to tie in the arts and STEM and have your students create an artifact to represent their global project.

Foster Grandparent Program

Jerry's middle school had a unique Health Careers Program, and one of the components was a Foster Grandparent Program. The students visited a health facility, senior center, or nursing home once a week during the school year. They adopted one of the residents and spent some quality time with that person on their visit. Later the students discussed their Foster Grandparent Program experiences with other classes around the country.

It is wonderful to make personal connections and see that we all can learn from one another. Connecting older people with youngsters was an eye-opening experience for both age levels. Each group left with a better understanding of the other's unique perspectives. Your students can interact with their grandparents and gather oral histories of their lives and experiences. They can then share and compare their lives today with those of their older relatives or acquaintances.

E-Book

Teachers have connected with other classes to have their students jointly write **e-books**. Google Docs can enable both classes to collaborate easily. E-books cover a multitude of topics such as school subject areas, holidays, events, or student interests. A joint e-book can connect students in different countries. Some e-books contain not only text but pictures and multimedia creations as well.

Dreamwakers*

"DreamWakers is a nonprofit organization that harnesses the power of free video technologies like Skype and Google Hangout to bring exceptional career speakers into public school classrooms, inspiring students across America."[6] After teachers sign up, they are contacted by a dedicated working professional from DreamWakers' Career Corp.

Billy took part in this career education opportunity, and his students were able to learn from an Apple employee about career possibilities in the fields of art and technology.

Chapter Collaborative Credits

Dan Curcio
Meghan Everette

Resources

Blogging: www.cybraryman.com/blogs2.html
DreamWakers: www.dreamwakers.org
Email: www.cybraryman.com/email.html
Flat Stanley: www.cybraryman.com/primaryed.html#FlatStanley
Health Careers Program: www.cybraryman.com/hcp.html
Olympics: www.cybraryman.com/olympics.html
Ongoing Global Collaborative Projects: www.21stcenturyschools.com/global_col laborative_projects.htm#Ongoing%20Collaborative%20Projects
Science Fair: www.cybraryman.com/sciencefair.html
Scientists Help Science Teachers Using Social Media: www.dandanscienceman. com/scientists-help-science-teachers-using-social-media/
SCI-U-SHARE: www.dandanscienceman.com/sci-u-share/

The Next Chapter

In Chapter 4 we will explore holidays and events that take place in the fall season. It will provide teachers with ideas about how to celebrate them and then connect with other classes to enhance learning for their students.

Notes

1. www.youtube.com/watch?v=1sokhOOk2bg.
2. www.dandanscienceman.com/scientists-help-science-teachers-using-social-media/.
3. www.cybraryman.com/primaryed.html#FlatStanley.
4. Scholastic Teachers. (2015). Making connections with Flat Stanley: Framed in France. *Scholastic.com*. Retrieved 14 February 2015 from www.scholastic.com/teachers/top-teaching/2014/10/making-connections-flat-stanley-framed-france.
5. Ibid.
6. http://www.dreamwakers.org/#!the-dream/ceu8.

4

Fall Projects

As educators, we feel it is important that students understand different holidays and events that occur during the school year. In some cases students get days off from school and do not really know why. In this and the next two chapters we will show you ways to incorporate the seasons, holidays, events, and celebrations into your lessons and use them as a way to connect with other classes as well.

In this chapter we are going to explore different projects that we have participated in during the fall months or projects that we have heard about. These projects usually occur during the months of September, October, and November. Depending on where you are located, some of these projects might be a good way to kick off becoming a connected classroom. We have also included ideas on how to celebrate holidays and events that occur during this season.

This is meant to be a practical guide for finding projects that are useful and advice on different ways in which to start collaborating. These projects can be used as a follow-up to Mystery Location Calls or as separate projects that can be used to connect your students with other classrooms. The asterisk (*) indicates projects that we have participated in. If there is not an asterisk, these are ideas or suggestions that you could expand upon in your classroom.

Chapter 4: Fall Projects

September	**October**
Labor Day	Global Read Aloud (GRA)*
O.R.E.O. Project*	Fall—How Weather Affects Us*
September 11: Showing Compassion	Pumpkin Seed Project*
Hispanic Heritage	Halloween Projects
(September 15–October 15)	
International Dot Day* (September 15)	

November
Election Day
Veterans Day/Remembrance Day
Gettysburg Address*
Native American Heritage Month
Thanksgiving Day: Canada (October) vs. the United States (November)
Plimoth Plantation*

September Projects

Labor Day

(Common Core State Standards: RI.9, W.2, W.7, SL) (ISTE Standards for Students: 2, 3, 5, 6) (ISTE Standards for Teachers: 1, 2)

The preparation for this celebration of workers is a chance for classes to connect with people in different careers. All subject areas should be represented with in-person and online opportunities to meet workers and question them about their career preparation and job responsibilities. Connect with classes in other countries to determine when and how this holiday is celebrated where they live. Connecting with other classrooms in the United States might be more of a challenge for this holiday in light of the fact that not everyone starts school before **Labor Day**. Find out why other schools always start after Labor Day.

O.R.E.O. (Our Really Exciting Online) Project*

(Common Core State Standards: MD.1, MD.2, MD.9, CC, SL) (ISTE Standards for Students: 2, 3, 5, 6) (ISTE Teacher Standards: 1, 2, 3, 4)

Figure 4.1 Final results of the O.R.E.O Project.

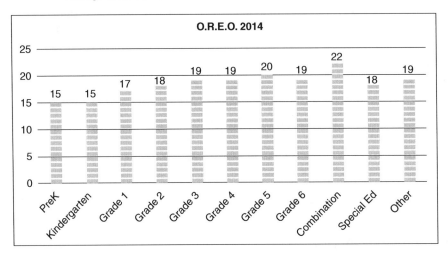

FINAL RESULTS AS OF OCTOBER 19, 2014

Classes Posting Results	542
# of Participants	14,074
Average Stack Count	18

The **O.R.E.O. Project** involves stacking Oreo cookies as high as you can, finding your class average, and submitting the results to a collaborative document. This is one of the many projects hosted by Jennifer Wagner (@jenwagner) since 1999. Her site has information about the 2014 O.R.E.O. Project.[1] Projects by Jen (www.projectsbyjen) is one site you should bookmark as a great starting place for your journey through collaborative projects.

Jen asks teachers interested in participating to register on her site. She gives the general guidelines for the stacking part of the project and encourages participating classes to reach out, connect, and do extension projects as part of the O.R.E.O. Project.

Paula challenges other classes to do the stacking against her class via Skype or Google Hangouts. Her classes have also shared the sculptures they made with other classes during the videoconferences. Her students have even had timed licking contests against other classes. Boy, is it fun to watch two classrooms full of students licking the icing off their Oreo cookies! They have shared their creative writings about Oreo cookies and had others solve the math problems they created involving the results of their Oreo stacking. To show force and motion, they build ramps with textbooks and cardboard and they roll their Oreo cookies to see how far they get.

They also measure and weigh the cookies and icing and put their results into graphs.

September 11: Showing Compassion

(Common Core State Standards: RI.6, RL.1, W.1, W.2, W.3, SL) (ISTE Standards for Students: 2, 3, 5, 6) (ISTE Standards for Teachers: 1, 2, 3, 4)

Find out how different communities in the United States and in other countries commemorate the attack on the United States that took place on **September 11, 2001**. This also presents a chance for students to connect with people who experienced this event personally or those willing to share their reaction to what happened on that day. Try to connect with people and get their feelings about the events that occurred in New York City, Washington, DC, and Western Pennsylvania. Jerry, in a Skype call, was interviewed by a class about where he was and how he felt upon learning what happened on September 11. The call also covered Jerry's reactions to President Kennedy's assassination on November 22, 1963, and to the space shuttle *Challenger* disaster on January 28, 1986.

Hispanic Heritage Month (September 15–October 15)

(Common Core State Standards: RI.6, RL.1, W.2, SL) (ISTE Standards for Students: 2, 3, 5, 6) (ISTE Standards for Teachers: 1, 2, 3, 4)

Each year in the United States, National **Hispanic Heritage Month** is observed from September 15 to October 15. There are many ways to celebrate the histories, cultures, and contributions of American citizens whose ancestors came from Spain, Mexico, the Caribbean, and Central and South America. The Latin American countries of Costa Rica, El Salvador, Guatemala, Honduras, and Nicaragua observe their independence anniversary on September 15. Mexico celebrates its independence on September 16, while Chile celebrates its independence on September 18.

Columbus Day, October 12, also falls within this 30-day period. This is a good opportunity to connect a class in a Spanish-speaking country with a class in a non-Spanish-speaking country. Have students come up with questions about their school day, culture, customs, holidays, history, and traditions. Carrying out these conversations can lead to collaborations in all subject areas.

International Dot Day* (September 15)

(Common Core State Standards: RL.1, RL.2, RL.3, RL.6, RL.7, W.6, SL, CC, MD) (ISTE Standards for Students: 2, 3, 5, 6) (ISTE Standards for Teachers: 1, 2, 3, 4)

How will you make your mark on September 15? International **Dot Day** is based on Peter H. Reynolds's book *The Dot*.[2] Terry Shay, a teacher in Iowa, decided to start this project after reading Reynolds's book to his class in 2009. Just like the main character in the book, students are encouraged to make their mark and share it with the world.

Terry has created a website, International Dot Day, where you can register and find a wealth of ideas and materials to help you and your students be part of this international project.[3] In 2014, Dot Day had almost two million participants from 85 different countries.

When author Sharon Creech (*Love That Dog, Walk Two Moons*) sent Terry her dot in 2011, he started the Celebri-dot site.[4] This is where he posts dots created by authors, sports figures, actors, and other celebrities who want to leave their mark.

Paula invited Rachel Schmidt's pre-K class to join her fourth graders for the festivities during the closing event of her 2014 Dot Day collaboration. The older students led the little ones through a series of stations they had set up in their classroom. Using bingo stampers, Paula's students helped their little buddies write their name with dots. They used a collection of dot-shaped objects to help the pre-K kids create collage-type pictures. Then all the students took turns playing Twister.

Paula's class also Skyped with author Laurie Ann Thompson (@LaurieThompson), and they played Mystery Skype with her to learn that she is located in Washington. They also did a Skype call with the famous storyteller Mrs. P (@MrsPstoryTime, Kathy Kinney) from California. Mrs. P shared her Celebri-dot[5] with the students and they shared their creations with her. The two classes ended their Dot Day celebration by eating donut holes and Dots candies.

A couple of years ago, Paula, who teaches in Louisiana, had a different kind of Dot Day collaboration. She was invited to Skype into Marialice BFX Curran's (@mbfxc) class of pre-service teachers in Connecticut to explain how she collaborates with other classrooms. Paula shared her students' dot creations and told how her class had shared their dots during the day with their Skype buddy class in Kansas.

Figure 4.2 International Dot Day Project.

Classrooms from around the world have connected and collaborated with others via videoconferencing, building **wikis** and web pages, and sharing blog posts and videos to celebrate how they left their mark on International Dot Day.

October Projects

Global Read Aloud (GRA)*

(Common Core State Standards: RL, W, SL) (ISTE Standards for Students: 1, 2, 3, 5, 6) (ISTE Standards for Teachers: 1, 2, 3, 4)

October starts off with a great collaborative read-aloud project. Pernille Ripp (@pernilleripp), a fifth-grade teacher in Wisconsin, started this project in 2010. It has grown to include over 500,000 participants from 60 different countries, who come together through different venues to read a novel or do an author study based on grade levels. Teachers can sign up on the official **Global Read**

Aloud site (www.theglobalreadaloud.com) and then choose the book they will read with their students. From there the teachers decide how they will connect their class to others through the myriad of platforms offered—Edmodo, Skype, Google Hangouts, email exchange, videos, **VoiceThread**, and more. This project runs for a six-week period and can definitely lead classes to other ways they can keep connecting and collaborating throughout the school year.

Story from a Member of Our PLN

Jennifer Regruth, one of the members of the Sunday Night Google Hangout, relays how her class used the **Padlet** tool to read *The Fourteenth Goldfish* for the Global Read Aloud in 2014.

> The #GRA2014, Global Read Aloud is underway! We are all enjoying the book and the kids are full of ideas about what will happen next. The book has done a good job of giving us descriptions of the characters, so the students have done a great job creating predictions.
>
> We decided to use a tool called Padlet to share our thoughts and predictions with other classrooms. I created a new Padlet and shared the link with the kids and away they went! They even figured out how to add pictures.
>
> We connected via GHO with another classroom to share our predictions. They students loved being on camera sharing their ideas with other 4th grade students. We are looking forward to connecting with them again at the end of the book to see if our predictions were accurate. These creative kiddos were full of great ideas![6]

Takeaways from Jennifer's Story

Figure out which web tool you can use to extend a project. Creating a Padlet allows your students' work to be easily shared with others. Others can even add to your Padlet. Connecting with other classrooms who are involved in the same project allows your students to share their thoughts and ideas beyond your classroom walls.

How Weather Affects Us*

(Common Core State Standards: W, SL, MD.4, MD.10, NBT.1, OA.1, OA.2) (Next Generation Science Standards: ESS2D, ESS3C, ESS3D, LS1, LS2) (ISTE Standards for Students: 1, 2, 3, 4, 5, 6) (ISTE Standards for Teachers: 1, 2, 3, 4)

The fall season is a chance for classes experiencing the changing of leaf colors to compare notes with other students around the country and the world who do not experience this seasonal change. The science behind the changing of leaf colors (**photosynthesis**) can be explored. Classes in different parts of the world can share the difference in climate and compare temperatures.

Paula (in Louisiana), Billy (in New Jersey), and Nancy Carroll, a fourth-grade teacher in Massachusetts, spent several Sunday evenings putting together a collaborative project for their classes by doing Google Hangouts with each other. The project they created was called "How Weather Affects Us."

Paula's students created surveys about weather using Google forms. By tweeting out the **URL**s to their surveys, they were able to collect weather data from many states in the United States and from countries including Great Britain, New Zealand, and Abu Dhabi. The three classes then held Skype calls to discuss the data and decided to create poster graphs in their math classes. Billy's students did a Google Hangout to show Paula's students how to enter the data into Excel spreadsheets to create online graphs.

Pumpkin Seed Project*

(Common Core State Standards: RI, W, SL, NBT, OA.1, MD.4, MD.10) (Next Generation Science Standards: LS1, LS2) (ISTE Standards for Students: 1, 2, 3, 5, 6) (ISTE Standards for Teachers: 1, 2, 3, 4)

During the last week in October, you'll want to check out the Pumpkin Seed Project. This is another collaborative project hosted by Jen Wagner on her Projects by Jen site. Although she only offers it to grades pre-K through 3, she encourages other grade levels to join in. Here is an example of how Paula used this project to jump-start The Great Pumpkin Seed Project with her fourth graders.[7] They then made Skype calls to share their information with other classes.

Halloween Projects

(Common Core State Standards: RI, RL, W.3) (ISTE Standards for Students: 1, 2, 3, 4, 5, 6) (ISTE Standards for Teachers: 1, 2, 3, 4)

Halloween provides the opportunity to have your students be very creative. Have them write a trick-or-treat or scary story, put on a play, or make a movie. You can also do a multimedia project that gives younger children important safety information for when they go trick or treat. Share your projects and work with another class via Google Docs to connect and create a joint activity.

November Projects

Election Day

(Common Core State Standards: RI, W.3, SL, NBT.4, OA.1, CC) (ISTE Standards for Students: 1, 2, 3, 5, 6) (ISTE Standards for Teachers: 1, 2, 3, 4)

The issues raised in political campaigns provide an opportunity to have an online debate between classes in different localities. A Google Hangout can be used not only to have the classes shown but to allow for judges to view the proceedings. **Virtual debates** are becoming more popular. Connect with a class in another school and do a mock campaign for office. Have students give two-minute speeches. If possible do this for class elections. Have each opposing class vote for who they would want for class officers in the other class based on their speeches. It would be interesting to see who the other class would elect for positions not really knowing the candidates, which could help remove the popularity aspect of class elections.

Veterans Day/Remembrance Day

(Common Core State Standards: RI.6, W.2, SL) (ISTE Standards for Students: 2, 3, 5) (ISTE Standards for Teachers: 1, 2, 3, 4)

To honor those who have served while allowing children to gain knowledge of the wars and conflicts our countries have been involved in, this holiday allows for connections with veterans. Local veterans' organizations can bring together students and veterans willing to be interviewed by students. These interviews can be conducted via a Skype call or in a Google Hangout.

Connect with classes in Canada, England, or Australia to learn how they celebrate **Remembrance Day** and then compare it to the way Veterans Day is celebrated in the United States.

Gettysburg Address*

(Common Core State Standards: RI, SL) (ISTE Standards for Students: 2, 3, 5) (ISTE Standards for Teachers: 1, 2, 3, 4)

In the fall of 2013, Billy did a Google Hangout with schools in California and Tennessee to honor the 150th anniversary of the Gettysburg Address. Students from each class read a section of the address for the others on a Google Hangout. This was another project hosted by Jen Wagner. The students were interested in celebrating this milestone event and were excited to connect with other classes. Students not only recited the Gettysburg Address but also asked each other questions about the significance of this historical document.

Native American Heritage Month

(Common Core State Standards: RI.6, RL.1, W.2, SL) (ISTE Standards for Students: 2, 3, 5, 6) (ISTE Standards for Teacher: 1, 2, 3, 4)

When Jerry went to elementary school, each year some Hopi Indians came to his school and talked about their customs and culture. It was quite fascinating to learn about them. Jerry made it a point to teach his students about the Native American tribe that inhabited the land in what is now their school neighborhood. Have your students do research to find out the Native American tribes that lived in their towns or cities. Then take the next step by reaching out to connect with members of that tribe. You can also do a Mystery Tribe Call with another class and have them try to determine the Native American tribe you are describing.

Thanksgiving Day: Canada (October) vs. the United States (November)

(Common Core State Standards: RI.6, W.2, SL) (ISTE Standards for Students: 2, 3, 5, 6) (ISTE Standards for Teachers: 1, 2, 3, 4)

Connect classes in Canada with those in the United States to discuss why and how Thanksgiving is celebrated in these two countries at different times in the fall. Many countries celebrate harvest festivals. Have your students discover how other countries celebrate harvests and then try to connect with classes in those countries to compare and contrast.

Plimoth Plantation*

(Common Core State Standards: RI, W, SL) (ISTE Standards for Students: 2, 3, 5) (ISTE Standards for Teachers: 1, 2, 3, 4, 5)

What better way to learn about **Plimoth Plantation** than to take a Virtual Field Trip there (we go into depth about Virtual Field Trips in Chapter 7). Billy was able to connect with Nancy Carroll to bring his students along with Nancy's students as they visited Plimoth Plantation. Nancy explained how she was able to share her field trip virtually:

> Using my smartphone and Skype, the class wandered in and out of the Plimoth Village (in real-time) and had several opportunities to listen to the Pilgrims as they spoke with my students. Questions from the New Jersey students were relayed to the Pilgrims via my students (as folks in the 1620's would never have understood a smartphone never mind Skype!).

Resources

Celebri-dots: www.celebridots.com
Civil War (Gettysburg): www.cybraryman.com/civilwar.html
Debate: www.cybraryman.com/debate.html
Dot Day: www.cybraryman.com/dotday.html
Election Day: www.cybraryman.com/elections.html
Fall: www.cybraryman.com/fall.html
Global Read Aloud: www.globalreadaloud.com/2014/11/sign-up-for-global-read-aloud-2015-gra15.html
The Great Pumpkin Project (Ms. Naugle): www.bit.ly/16lTwu0
Halloween:www.cybraryman.com/halloween.html
Harvest Festivals from Around the World: www.harvestfestivals.net/harvestfestivals.htm
Hispanic Heritage: www.cybraryman.com/hispanic.html

International Dot Day: www.thedotclub.org/dotday
Labor History: www.cybraryman.com/laborhistory.html
Laurie Ann Thompson: www.twitter.com/lauriethompson
Mrs. P's Magic Library: www.mrsp.com
Native Americans: www.cybraryman.com/nativeamericans.html
Plimoth Plantation: www.plimoth.org
Projects by Jen (Wagner): www.projectsbyjen.com
September 11: www.cybraryman.com/september11.html
Thanksgiving: www.cybraryman.com/thanksgiving.html
Veteran's Day/Remembrance Day:www.cybraryman.com/veteransday.html

The Next Chapter

In Chapter 5 we will explore ways to celebrate holidays and events that occur during the winter season and possible ways to connect your students with other classes. It will provide teachers with ideas on how to celebrate and enhance students' education.

Notes

1 www.projectsbyjen.com/Projects/OR2014/OP14_information.html.
2 www.peterhreynolds.com/dot/.
3 www.thedotclub.org/dotday/.
4 www.celebridots.com.
5 www.celebridots.com/2013/09/mrs-p-kathy-kinney.html.
6 www.brownroom18.blogspot.com/2014/10/our-padlet-for-fourteenth-goldfish.html#sthash.x3r4uDPB.dpuf.
7 www.bit.ly/16ITwu0.

5

Winter Projects

The winter season lends itself to many ways to connect with classes all over the world to talk about climate and weather conditions. Math and science activities can include movement of the Earth, temperature, wind chill, precipitation, composition of snow, amount of snow, lake-effect snow, polar vortex, and animals' hibernation and movement during winter. Compare the winter activities you enjoy doing with the activities of students in other areas of this country and around the world. What would be interesting is connecting with classes who have the opposite seasons. For example the Australian seasons are opposite of those in the northern hemisphere.

In this chapter we will also take a look at some heartfelt projects that are amazing and teach children about giving back to their communities. We will explore various projects that can be done during the holiday season to help students relate to the world.

We are going to explore different projects that we have participated in during the winter months and projects that we have heard about. These projects usually occur during the months of December, January, February, and March. Depending on your location, some of these projects might be a good way to kick off becoming a connected classroom. We have also included ideas about how to celebrate holidays and events that happen during this season.

Chapter 5: Winter Projects
*100th Day of School**

December	January
Holiday Card Exchange*	New Year's
RACK—Random Acts of Christmas/	Dr. Martin Luther King Jr.*
Holiday Kindness*	Martin's Big Words*
Pearl Harbor Day	
12.12.12 Blogging Challenge*	

February	March
American Heart Month*	Mardi Gras*
Black History Month*	Read Across America—Dr. Seuss's
Groundhog Day	Birthday*
Super Bowl Connections*	Commonwealth Day
Presidents' Day	Pi Day—March 14 (3/14)
Snow Days	St. Patrick's Day*
	Women's History Month

This is meant to be a practical guide for finding useful projects and ways to start collaborating in different ways. These projects can be used as a follow-up to Mystery Location Calls or as separate projects to connect your students with other classrooms. The asterisk (*) indicates projects that we have participated in. If there is not an asterisk (*), you could expand upon these ideas or suggestions in your classroom.

100th Day of School*

(As for the Common Core State Standards, many different standards could fit here depending upon the project. These are a few we suggest.) (Common Core State Standards: RI.5, W.4, W.5, W.6, SL, CC, NBT, OA, MD, G) (ISTE Standards for Students: 2, 3, 5, 6) (ISTE Standards for Teachers: 1, 2, 3, 4)

The commemoration of the **100th day of school** occurs at different times depending upon the first day of school where you live. There are many creative ways to celebrate this event. Connect with other classes to find out what they will be doing on this day. Share different ways to celebrate the 100th day of school in all subject areas. Find a class on Skype or Google

Hangouts and have a joint celebration. Students can discuss how they counted to 100 days of schools or they can share 100 facts about their town, city, or state. Have older students write a 100-word poem or song about school.

December Projects

Holiday Card Exchange*

(Common Core State Standards: W.4, W.5, W.6, SL) (ISTE Standards for Students: 2, 3, 5, 6) (ISTE Standards for Teachers: 1, 2, 3, 4)

The Holiday Card Exchange is another Project by Jen[1] and a fun learning experience for students. Teachers register on Jen Wagner's site and she makes groups consisting of 30 classrooms across North America. Each classroom can design their own card or each student can design a different holiday card staying within the theme. The classroom teacher is responsible for making sure there are enough cards to send out to all 29 other classrooms. During the 2014 Holiday Card Exchange, each class was asked to make one extra card and mail it to a local community service organization.

Each year the Holiday Card Exchange has a different theme, which makes it more exciting for the students. Billy uses one of his third-grade classes and has the students create holiday cards on computers. Paula has her students create handmade cards. One way that students learn about the world is by pinning on a map of North America the city each card comes from as it arrives. Some teachers have taken this to a new level using technology integration and created a Google map showing the locations of all of the other schools. Students then learn about the geographic location of the cities and different parts of the United States.

The Holiday Card Exchange enables students to learn geography, practice writing skills, use technology, and be as creative as they want when they design cards based on the annual theme. This is a great simple project to get students to start collaborating.

Figure 5.1 Holiday cards from around the world on display.

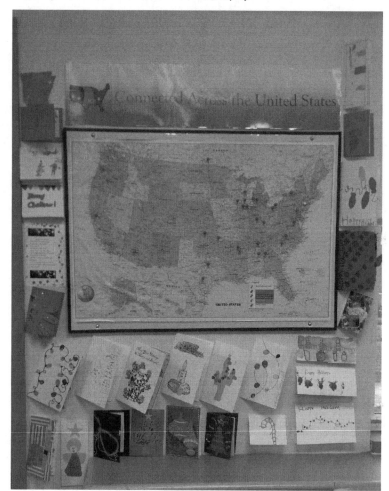

RACK—Random Acts of Christmas Kindness*

(Common Core State Standards: RI.6, W.5, W.6, W.7, SL) (ISTE Student Standards: 1, 2, 3, 4, 5, 6) (ISTE Standards for Teachers: 1, 2, 3, 4)

Teaching your students the true meaning of the holiday season is easy when you invite them to participate in RACK activities. Whereas Paula's students do this during the month of December, others prefer to do random acts of kindness and tie them in with Valentine's Day in February.

Paula loves the creative ideas her students come up with to "RACK" others in their school.

Have your students brainstorm kind acts they could do for others during this time of year. There are many lists and free printables you can attach to small tokens to be found on Pinterest[2] and there's even a Facebook page to help you get started.[3]

Find some other classes (maybe just in your building) to share your RACK experiences using videoconferencing or an Edmodo group or through blogging. Invite other teachers to sign up via a Google Doc for a virtual RACK activity. Then, on their day, present them with a special holiday treat by having your students sing them carols, read them holiday stories, recite seasonal poems, or present a Christmas play.

Pearl Harbor Day

(Common Core State Standards: RI.6, RL.1, RL.3, RL.6, W.2, W.4, W.5, W.6, W.9, SL, MD) (ISTE Student Standards: 1, 2, 3, 4, 5, 6) (ISTE Standards for Teachers: 2, 3, 4)

December 7, 1941, is a fateful day in American history, the day Japan attacked the naval base at Pearl Harbor in Hawaii. Have students do some research on the events of this day and try to connect with older adults who remember this event and get their reaction to what transpired as a result of this attack. The same can be done for other important dates in history such as President Kennedy's assassination, the *Challenger* explosion, and September 11. Students can be connected to other students in programs such as Edmodo, **Google Classroom**, and VoiceThread to discuss these events and take different viewpoints.

12.12.12 Blogging Challenge*

(Common Core State Standards: W.3, W.5, W.6, SL) (ISTE Standards for Students: 1, 2, 3, 4, 5, 6) (ISTE Standards for Teachers: 1, 2, 3, 4)

In December 2012, after taking part in many of Jen Wagner's projects for several years, Paula was inspired by her mentor and decided to host her own collaborative project.

She decided to invite other teachers who had their students blogging to take part in the 12.12.12 Blogging Challenge. Using a Google Form, she asked teachers to register prior to December 12 and put the URL to their students' blogs in the form. Then on December 12, the students were to write a blog post about 12 things of their choosing. The topics ranged from their 12 favorite books to their 12 most cherished possessions. Some students chose to create a list, while one student posted 12 videos of his favorite hockey moments. One of my favorites is a blog post by Raf from Russia, who decided to write 12 sentences about himself.[4] Students were encouraged to visit the blogs of others who participated in the challenge and to leave comments.

While December 12, 2012, has come and gone, consider hosting your own blogging challenge. It could be set up to coincide with a special date:

♦ 10/10: My Ten Greatest Accomplishments
♦ 11/11: Eleven Things You Don't Know about Me
♦ 12/12: My Twelve Favorite ___
♦ 3/3: The Best Three Books I've Ever Read and Why
♦ 4/4: Four Things on My Bucket List before School Ends

Let your imagination soar! Ask your students what blogging challenge they would like to host. Then get ready to collaborate. I would encourage you to set up a Google Form for others to register and tweet about your challenge well in advance. You could set up a Remind class for the participants and send out text reminders of the approaching date. When the date arrives, plan to videoconference with some of the participating classes. Tweet about the dates and times your class is available and keep a Google Doc of the connections you would like to make.

January Projects

New Year's

(Common Core State Standards: W.3, SL) (ISTE Standards for Students: 2, 3, 4, 5) (ISTE Standards for Teachers: 1, 2, 3, 4)

The New Year provides a wonderful opportunity to connect your class with another in a foreign country to find out how they celebrate this day. Include in your discussions with these students making resolutions and how to keep them.

Dr. Martin Luther King Jr.*

> *(Common Core State Standards: RI.6, W.2, W.7, SL) (ISTE Standards for Students: 2, 3, 4, 5, 6) (ISTE Standards for Teachers: 1, 2, 3, 4)*

There are many different ways you can connect with other classrooms about Dr. Martin Luther King Jr. One way is to organize an online short speech competition with another class with the theme of civil rights using nonviolent civil disobedience as practiced by Dr. King. Using a Google Hangout, you can have a panel of judges from other locations decide which class won. Connect through various websites such as Edmodo, Google Classroom, or VoiceThread; allow students to share essays based on the theme "I Have a Dream" or let them collaborate on a speech they would give.

Martin's Big Words*

> *(Common Core State Standards: RI.1, SL) (ISTE Standards for Students: 2, 5, 6) (ISTE Standards for Teachers: 2, 3, 4)*

In 2013, Billy worked with Connie Fink on a collaborative project about the civil rights movement. This project involved a third-grade class and a sixth-grade class; the students discussed the civil rights movement using the book *Martin's Big Words*. The questions and quotes that were discussed follow:

> Why do you think these "white only" signs were present in Southern cities and towns in the United States?
>
> Who was Mahatma Gandhi and how did he influence the civil rights movement in the United States?
>
> *Martin's Big Words*: "Hate cannot drive out hate. Only love can do that."
>
> How would people react today if they were sitting next to Rosa Parks and she was asked to "get up from her seat"? What makes today's reaction different from 1955?
>
> Why was the strategy *not* to ride "buses until they could sit anywhere they wanted" a good one (boycotting)? Did it follow Gandhi's way of thinking?
>
> Wow, 381 days! Would you be able/willing to walk to school in the "rain and cold and in blistering heat"? In what ways did Dr. Martin Luther King Jr. walking and talking with them, singing and praying, give the African Americans strength?

Martin's Big Words: "Wait! For years I have heard the word 'Wait!' We
   have waited more than 340 years."
Martin's Big Words: "Love is the key to the problems of the world."
Martin's Big Words: "Remember, if I am stopped, this movement will
   not be stopped, because God is with this movement."
"He won it because he taught others to fight with words not fists."
   What can we learn in our own lives from this thought?
"His big words are alive for us today." What can we do to continue to
   keep his words alive today?

February Projects

American Heart Month*

*(Common Core State Standards: RI.6, W.2, CC, NBT, MD) (ISTE Standards
for Students: 2, 5) (ISTE Standards for Teachers: 2, 3, 4)*

The prevention of heart disease should start with our adolescents. There is
an epidemic of obesity and other unhealthy habits among our youth. We
need to get young people thinking about ways to be healthy. Jerry enjoys
passing an elementary school and watching students jogging around the
campus. He likes seeing a middle school that has a Mile Club and remem-
bering his own children having to do a mile run. Find out what other
schools are doing about keeping fit. Set up discussions of healthy habits
and then start competitions between two classes in different locations via
Skype or Google Hangouts. Have students set up a spreadsheet to keep
track of the distance they walk or run each day. Show them apps they can
use on their mobile devices to track their fitness. Involve parents and work
with them on ways to keep their children fit.

Physical education departments in many schools have students compete in Jump Rope for Heart during this time of the year as well. At Paula's
school the students post graphs in the main lobby to show how much
money each grade level has collected. Younger students love graphing
how many jumps they do each day for the week. Older students keep track
of their heart rate before and after jumping rope. To make Jump Rope for
Heart a collaborative project, send out a tweet or Facebook post asking for
a partner school with which to compare results. Connect the classrooms via
Skype or Google Hangouts and let the students share their results, demonstrate their best jump-roping skills, or sing their favorite jump-rope songs.

Black History Month*

(Common Core State Standards: RI.6, W.2, W.3, W.4, W.5, W.6, W.7, SL) (ISTE Standards for Students: 1, 2, 3, 4, 5, 6) (ISTE Standards for Teachers: 1, 2, 3, 4)

February is celebrated as Black History Month. Engage another class in a competition to determine if they can figure out the famous black person you are describing. This activity will be similar to the Olympics challenge we did with several classes. It was a fun challenge where clever questions were raised and so much was learned. Share information about famous black people in your town, city, state, and country with other classes around the country or the world. Have your students prepare reports about a famous living black person. This will enhance their research skills and their ability to find accurate information from reliable sources.

Groundhog Day

(Common Core State Standards: RI.6, W.6, W.7, SL, MD.4, MD.9) (Next Generation Science Standards: ESS2, ESS3) (ISTE Standards for Students: 1, 2, 3, 4, 5, 6) (ISTE Standards for Teachers: 1, 2, 3, 4)

The yearly Groundhog Day event on February 2 is an opportunity to learn about the seasons, climate, light, shadows, and solar observations. Have the classes do some research on the location of Punxsutawney, Pennsylvania, and the accuracy of their statistics throughout the years. Reach out to classes in other locations to compare daily weather and climate. Have students keep daily charts of sunrise, sunset, temperature, and other weather facts. Each class should then offer their own predictions and periodically connect with the other class to see how their predictions have turned out. These connections can be used through a variety of formats; Edmodo, Google Classroom, Google Docs, and VoiceThread are just a few tools with which students can use to collaborate.

Super Bowl Connections*

(Common Core State Standards: RI.6, W.6, W.7, SL, MD.4, MD.9) (ISTE Standards for Students: 2, 3, 4, 5, 6) (ISTE Standards for Teachers: 1, 2, 3, 4)

In 2012 when the New York Giants and New England Patriots both reached the Super Bowl, Billy (from New Jersey, a fan of the New York Giants) and Nancy (from Massachusetts, a fan of the New England Patriots) had their very first Mystery Skype Call the Monday after both teams made it into the Super Bowl. As the Mystery Skype Call went on and the two classes discovered each other's location, they realized that Billy's school was within a ten-minute drive of Giants Stadium and that Nancy's school was almost across the street from Gillette Stadium. At that point, Nancy and Billy decided to connect their classes beyond the Mystery Skype Call and that the classes would do something related to the Super Bowl.

After much discussion the two decided to learn all about the state in which the Super Bowl was taking place. That year it was Indianapolis, Indiana. Nancy and Billy had their classes explore different facts about the state. The students learned about the geography, demographics, natural features, resources, products, and borders of Indiana. They also learned more about the city of Indianapolis. The two classes met again on the Friday before the Super Bowl and shared what they had learned. The students in both classes wore their home teams' jerseys. It was a great way to have the students connect beyond the Mystery Skype Call, and of course the classes did have a little wager going on. As a result, Nancy had a Giants pennant hanging in her classroom for the rest of the school year.

Sports are great ways to use mathematics in education because math is applied constantly in all sporting events. Math provides opportunities to study player and team statistics, distances, probability, and percentages. You can have students determine how many more yards a player needs to run to get a first down, or the percentage of caught passes thrown by the quarterback, or how much time has elapsed in the game. Mathematics is in all sports, so this is a great way to engage those students who might have a huge interest in sports but don't see the connection between sports and what they are learning in school. Children can try to guess the final score of a football game using different variations of touchdowns, field goals, safeties, extra points, and even missed extra points. Have students find the statistics on their favorite players on the major sports leagues pages and compare them to other similar players.

Here is a story about the National Football League Playoff to decide who would go to the Super Bowl from one of our PLN members, Jennifer Regruth. She made a connection through Nancy Carroll, another #4thchat participant. Nancy's former principal teaches at a school right across from the Patriots stadium. He was initiating a program to connect with other schools near the stadium where the Patriots were playing to promote good sportsmanship. Jennifer set up the connection with a fourth-grade class-room in Massachusetts and planned a time to have a Google Hangout. The teachers collaborated and decided to use math to guess the score, and each side came up with different ways to get that score. For example, if Jennifer's school in Indiana picked the score of 24–21 for a Colts win, did they get the points through touchdowns, extra points, field goals, or safeties? The students had fun guessing. Each school was wearing the gear of their favorite team and showing handmade signs to support their team. The students and teachers wished each other luck. The two classes actually connected twice because they did a video chat during the regular season and then again in the playoffs. As demonstrated by Jennifer's story, you can also apply mathematics to an event like the National Football League Playoffs and make the event more educationally meaningful to the students.

Another great project to do during the Super Bowl is the "Souper Bowl of Caring," an event that takes place around the same time as the Super Bowl, where students collect cans of soup to donate to local food pantries. You can connect with other classrooms participating in this national program and have a friendly competition. You can graph the number of cans your students collect daily, break down the different types of soups that you have collected, and take a survey of students' favorite soups. All of these activities can be done both in your school and with other classrooms across the United States. For more information about the "Souper Bowl of Caring," visit www.souperbowl.org/.

Presidents' Day

(Common Core State Standards: RI.6, W.2, W.4, W.5, W.6, W.7, SL) (ISTE Standards for Students: 1, 2, 3, 4, 5, 6) (ISTE Standards for Teachers: 1, 2, 3, 4)

Connect with another class and discuss the characteristics of a good leader. Compare types of government with classes around the world. Find out the different forms of government in your town and city and what leaders are needed. Invite a local leader into your classroom in person or via Skype or Google Hangouts. Have your students do some research and then plan appropriate questions beforehand. Carry out an interview with the leader. Divide your students into different groups to work with other classrooms from around the country in Google Classroom or Edmodo. Post questions to one another and have them research the questions. Create a multimedia project on the US presidents using their quotations and sound clips of them. You can also put together some fun facts and historical details. Have students conduct mock interviews of a famous president. Have students use a program such as Tech4Learning Frames to record and animate the character.

Snow Days

(Common Core State Standards: W.3, W.6, OA, MD) (Next Generation Science Standards: ESS2, ESS3) (ISTE Standards for Students: 2, 4, 5, 6) (ISTE Standards for Teachers: 1, 2, 3, 4)

Days off from school because of inclement weather are opportunities for students to work on blog posts and connect to their classmates in a global group by leaving comments on the blogs of students in other locations. A good way to find blogs for this activity is through the hashtag #comments4kids on Twitter. Teachers all over the globe will tweet out their students' blog URLs, inviting comments from others.

If you use Edmodo, create a collaborative group within it and share the code with the classes you connect with throughout the year. Have students come up with interesting learning projects they would like to do on days when school is closed and post them to your Edmodo collaborative group. Days off from school are perfect opportunities to extend the learning of your students and also gives them more time to follow their passions.

Another option is to create a shared Google Doc where students can write about what they did on their "snow day," which could be shared via social media for others to collaborate on as well.

March Projects

Mardi Gras*

(Common Core State Standards: RI.6, W.2, W.4, W.5., W.6, SL) (ISTE Standards for Students: 2, 3, 5, 6) (ISTE Standards for Teachers: 1, 2, 3, 4)

Mardi Gras is a unique celebration, and many students do not know the true meaning behind it. Paula teaches in New Orleans and has had her

Figure 5.2 A tweet that Billy sent out after the Mardi Gras event in 2012.

Billy Krakower
@wkrakower

@plnaugle My students loved your students Mardi Gras presentation. Thanks for including us.

8:01 PM - 10 Feb 2012

students do research on different aspects of Mardi Gras. During the two weeks leading up to this celebration, Paula's students share their firsthand experience with other classes. Paula invites other classrooms to learn about Mardi Gras through Skype or Google Hangouts. She sends out a Google Form for classes to sign up so they can come into her class and learn. This is a great example of ways to share the learning experience from your classroom with other classrooms.

Linda Yollis wrote a blog post about the time she participated in the Mardi Gras Skype Call in 2012.[5] Patti Grayson also posted about the Mardi Gras Skype Call.[6]

Read Across America—Dr. Seuss's Birthday

(Depending upon the project selected you can apply a number of Common Core State Standards.) (Common Core State Standards: RL, SL) (ISTE Standards for Students: 2, 5, 6) (ISTE Standards for Teachers: 1, 2, 3, 4)

As part of **Read Across America,** Jerry had the distinct pleasure to read *The Cat in the Hat Comes Back* to classes in Indiana, Louisiana, Massachusetts, Michigan, New Jersey, and Pennsylvania as part of a Google Hangout. This special event was also seen by classes all over the world on YouTube. Jerry shared many interesting facts about Dr. Seuss because he spent a lot of time in Seuss's hometown of Springfield, Massachusetts, where Jerry's wife also grew up. This was a great way for the students involved to expand their connections from Mystery Location Calls, as most of the classes had previously participated in such calls together (Blumengarten, 2013).

Commonwealth Day

(Common Core State Standards: W, SL) (ISTE Standards for Students: 2, 3, 4) (ISTE Standards for Teachers: 1, 2, 3, 4)

Commonwealth Day is a celebration of the Commonwealth of Nations that is held on the second Monday in March. It is also a chance to understand the cooperative work on Commonwealth organizations. Have your students do research on what countries constituted the Commonwealth of Nations and how they work together. Connect with classes that celebrate this annual event to find out more about it.

Pi Day—March 14 (3/14)

(Common Core State Standards: RI.6, RL.1, RL.5, W.2, W.7, SL, MD, G) (ISTE Standards for Students: 2, 3, 5, 6) (ISTE Standards for Teachers: 1, 2, 3, 4)

Pi Day (celebrated on March 14, to represent the value of π, 3.14) is a great way to do some cross-curricular work especially focusing on mathematics. Have your students come up with Pi Day activities that will appeal to all of their senses. Students can create learning board or computer games that involve the use of π. Connect with other classes to brainstorm ways to celebrate Pi Day with activities and projects in all subject areas. Read *Sir Cumference and the Dragon of Pi,* which is a great story to get the conversation started about what is π. There are a number of amazing stories in the Sir Cumference series as well.[7] Conduct surveys through various social media channels and have students create pi graphs. Students can share and analyze data during a Google Hangout or Skype call.

St. Patrick's Day*

(Common Core State Standards: RI, RL, W, SL, CC, OA, MD) (ISTE Standards for Students: 2, 3, 5, 6) (ISTE Standards for Teachers: 1, 2, 3, 4)

Ireland is rich in castles and their history. Students can learn about the history of Ireland and its legends, as well as facts and fiction about St. Patrick's

Day. Bring students to Ireland by visiting Castles of Northern Ireland on Virtual Visit Tours and taking virtual tours of the castles in Ireland.[8] Students can connect with other classrooms or write a blog post if they celebrate St. Patrick's Day and discuss family traditions around the holiday.

Jen Wagner also hosts a project targeted at pre-K through third grade called St. Patrick's Day Project, which has students use a box of Lucky Charms to categorize and count the marshmallow shapes found in the cereal. As with all of her projects, Jen encourages classes to find ways to connect and collaborate during the two weeks she runs the project.

Women's History Month

(Common Core State Standards: RL.1, RI.6, W.2, W.7, SL) (ISTE Standards for Students: 2, 3, 6) (ISTE Standards for Teachers: 1, 2, 3, 4)

In a spin-off of the Mystery Location Call in honor of Women's History Month, have your students come up with five-minute oral presentations on famous women. The students can dress up as the woman they chose to study if they wish. They should also respond to questions as if they were in that time period. Each class will take turns presenting, and the other class has to figure out who the mystery woman is. Each oral presentation should last around five minutes. Listening skills will be essential to help pick up on clues in each presentation. Researchers must be able to find accurate information quickly. Students should prepare for these Mystery Woman Calls by practicing their search skills along with their ability to evaluate information. Make sure to assign jobs for all the students in the class during the call. You will need researchers, questioners, and fact-checkers, as well as the normal Mystery Location Call jobs. Additionally, ensure that students report on why they chose this person to study.

Resources

100th Day of School: www.cybraryman.com/100thday1.html

Black History: www.cybraryman.com/blackhistory.html

Castles Northern Ireland, Virtual Visit Tours: www.virtualvisittours.com/category/castles-northern-ireland/

Chinese New Year: www.cybraryman.com/chinesenewyear.html

Civil Rights Movement: www.cybraryman.com/civilrights.html

Dr. Martin Luther King Jr.: www.cybraryman.com/mlk.html

Groundhog Day: www.cybraryman.com/groundhog.html

Mardi Gras: www.yollisclassblog.blogspot.com/2012/02/mardi-gras-learning-from-experts.html

New Year's: www.cybraryman.com/new_years.html

Pi Day: www.cybraryman.com/math.html

Presidents' Day: www.cybraryman.com/presidents.html

Resolutions: www.cybraryman.com/resolutions2.html

St. Patrick's Day: www.cybraryman.com/stpatrick.html and http://projectsbyjen.com/Projects/SP2015/sp2015Home.html

Super Bowl/Football: www.cybraryman.com/football.html

Valentine's Day: www.cybraryman.com/valentine.html

Winter/Snow Fun: www.cybraryman.com/snow.html

Women's History: www.cybraryman.com/women.html

The Next Chapter

In Chapter 6 we will explore ways to celebrate holidays and events that occur during the spring and summer seasons and possibilities for connecting your students with other classes. It will provide teachers with ideas for celebrations with their students and others across the country and the world.

Notes

1. www.projectsbyjen.com/Projects/HCE2014/HCE14Welcome.html.
2. www.pinterest.com/shandabauman/rack-random-acts-of-christmas-kindness/.
3. www.facebook.com/RACK.theworld.
4. 12 sentences about me, *Well Done! 2013/14*, www.kidblog.org/WellDone201213/d3578abc-82cb-4d48-b9a7-a8b01e2a1eb5/12-sentences-about-me/.
5. www.yollisclassblog.blogspot.com/2012/02/mardi-gras-learning-from-experts.html.
6. www.plpnetwork.com/2012/05/29/our-skype-adventures-creating-connected-learners-in-the-global-classroom/.
7. For more information about the series visit www.livingmath.net/Reviews/Reviews-ChildrensMathLit/SirCumferenceSeries/tabid/414/Default.aspx.
8. www.virtualvisittours.com/category/castles-northern-ireland/.

6

Spring and Summer Projects

In this chapter we are going to explore different projects that could be implemented during the spring and summer, ones we have either participated in or heard about. These projects usually occur during April, May, June, July, and August. We have also included ideas about how to celebrate holidays and events that occur during this season.

This is meant to be a practical guide for finding projects that are useful and ways in which to start collaborating. These projects can be used as a follow-up to Mystery Location Calls or as separate projects to connect your students with other classrooms. The asterisk (*) indicates projects that we have participated in. If there is not an asterisk (*),these are ideas or suggestions that you could expand upon in your classroom.

Spring Projects

April Projects

National Autism Awareness Month

(Common Core State Standards: RI.6, W.6, W.7, SL) (ISTE Standards for Students: 2, 3, 5, 6) (ISTE Standards for Teachers: 1, 2, 3, 4)

Chapter 6: Spring and Summer Projects

April
National Autism Awareness Month
Standardized Testing*
PictureIt Project*
Impromptu Calls*
Poetry Month*
April Fools' Day
Baseball
Holocaust Remembrance Day
Earth Day—Groceries Project*
Arbor Day

May	June
National Inventors Month	Flag Day
10-Day Passion Challenge and Identity Day*	Graduation—End of School
Cinco de Mayo*	
Memorial Day	

Have your students do research on autism. Arrange a connection with another class to allow your students share their knowledge about autism and help spread awareness and acceptance of those with autism and anyone who is different. Try to have an autism expert come into your class in person or virtually. Start an autism awareness campaign in your school led by your students. After reading such books as *Since We're Friends: An Autism Picture Book*, *I'm Here*, or *Different Like Me: My Book of Autism Heroes*, discuss what was learned and how everyone can be more understanding of students with developmental disabilities.

Standardized Testing*

(Common Core State Standards: RI.6, W, SL) (ISTE Standards for Students: 1, 2, 5, 6) (ISTE Standards for Teachers: 1, 2, 3, 4)

During the spring term students are faced with a lot of important tests. There is a great amount of stress associated with testing, so this is an opportunity to connect students in different schools and states to discuss ways to cope at this time of year. Work on a collaborative Google Document that includes ways to reduce this anxiety. Then take the information gained and produce a pamphlet that can be distributed to students and parents to help ease the testing anxiety.

You could also put together a video with test-taking strategies using clips from several different classrooms with which you are now connected. Students love being able to create, and allowing them to do so at this time will help alleviate some of their test anxiety.

PictureIt Project*

(Common Core State Standards: RI, SL, CC, MD, G) (ISTE Standards for Students: 2, 5, 6) (ISTE Standards for Teachers: 1, 2, 3, 4)

PictureIt is another great project hosted by Jen Wagner. It involves 24 classes with each class recreating 1/24th of a piece of art. Your class makes your square 24 times and then mails it out to your collaborative groups. It makes a beautiful visual to demonstrate how your class is connected to others. Classes have completed works of art by Monet, Van Gogh, and Mondrian over the past several years. In 2015, Jen is having the groups create a collaborative quilt instead of an art piece. You can check out pictures, blog posts, and videos of this project on Jen's archive page. Go to Projects by Jen (www.projectsbyjen.com/) to sign up for the current PictureIt project.

Impromptu Calls*

(As for the Common Core State Standards, many different standards could fit here depending upon the project—check RI, RL, W, SL) (ISTE Standards for Students: 1, 2, 5, 6) (ISTE Standards for Teachers: 1, 2, 3, 4, 5)

During one #4thchat on Twitter a couple of years ago, Paula started a discussion about doing impromptu Skype calls when standardized testing was over. She started a Google Doc and asked other interested teachers to sign up. They indicated which days they would be available to take an impromptu call. By keeping Skype open on their computer, they would know when a call was coming in. If they could take a video call, they would answer, and the two classes would chat with each other and bring each other up to date on what was happening in their classroom and in their community. These were great calls to make between classes that had connected during the year. The students shared their writings, their artwork, and their favorite movies, books, and games. One time a class even shared what made each person unique.

On one such Impromptu Skype call, Paula's class placed a call to Jan Wells, teacher of their Skype buddy class in Kansas, and was surprised when Jan answered because she had a classroom full of teachers instead of her students. She was conducting an in-service about using Skype to connect with other classes. What perfect timing! The students shared with these teachers the Earth Day grocery bags they had just finished decorating.

Doing Impromptu Skype calls or Impromptu Google Hangouts is a very relaxed way to keep your connections going. There is no advanced planning involved. You simply place the call and have a conversation. Think of all of the topics of conversation that you could initiate between two or more classes. They also are a great way to let students direct their own learning as they decide what topic of conversation they would like.

Poetry Month*

(Common Core State Standards: RI, RL, W, SL) (ISTE Standards for Students: 2, 5, 6) (ISTE Standards for Teachers: 1, 2, 3, 4)

Have your students either write their own poem or copy a favorite poem and put it in their pocket. This activity is part of Poetry Month's Poem in Your Pocket Day at the end of April. Poetry Month gives students the opportunity to create different types of poems, such as acrostic, blank verse, cinquain, free verse, haiku, limericks, lyric, narrative, rhyme, shape, tanka, and visual. Employ technology to produce the poems. Have a poetry slam (where students read their original poems) on a Google Hangout with several classes and use another class to judge them.

Here is a story about a poetry summit from Elissa Malespina (@elissa-malespina), a member of our PLN from New Jersey.

Two years ago the idea for a Poetry Summit started with ways to connect kids virtually and show their love of poetry. Frances Ann Squire from Birchwood Intermediate School on Prince Edward Island, Canada, Shawn Storm from Strayer Middle School in Quakertown, PA, Elissa Malespina and Melissa Butler from South

Orange Middle School in South Orange, New Jersey and Janelle Thompson and Shannon McClintock Miller from Van Meter Community School in Van Meter, Iowa, all came together to have students connect via Edmodo, and Google Hangout. During the Poetry Summit students not only read the poetry they created, but also got to hear poems from famous poets like Robert Forbes, and Tina Kelly. Ms. P from Ms. Ps storytime also made a guest appearance. During the second year of the summit, we expanded it from a 2 hour event to a full day event. We even added a kickoff event where we had a college professor come in and teach the students a lesson on creating poetry. Using Google Hangout, we recorded the event so that any school who was participating could use the lesson with their students even if they could not be there for the lesson in person. Many more schools participated in last years summit including some from Hawaii and Canada. The event also became international with the addition of the Shakespeare HipHop company who joined us from London, England. None of this would have been possible without technology like Google Hangout! Students still talk about the event to this day!

April Fools' Day

(Common Core State Standards: W.4, W.6, SL) (ISTE Standards for Students: 2, 5, 6) (ISTE Standards for Teachers: 1, 2, 3, 4)

Silly as it may seem, April Fools' Day presents many teaching opportunities in different subject areas. Jerry used to give his students a sheet with ten things to do in order. The instructions were to read the entire sheet before doing the exercise, but most students did not follow that direction; the last statement had them only do one task. It taught his students to read everything carefully and not be fooled easily. Find creative ways to use humor correctly in your classroom. Connect with other classes to creatively celebrate April Fools' Day.

Baseball

(Common Core State Standards: RI, RL, W, SL, NBT, MD, G) (ISTE Standards for Students: 1, 2, 3, 4, 5, 6) (ISTE Standards for Teachers: 1, 2, 3, 4)

The start of the baseball season lends itself to many different ways to celebrate this sport. Math plays a big part in baseball, and you can have students find and keep track of their favorite players and team statistics.

For social studies activities you can map the location and distances between cities of rival teams and find the derivation of your team's name. Connect with students in other areas of the country or Canada to play math or trivia baseball games of your making. Have students conduct research on the history of baseball and connect with students in states that are home to the original baseball teams. You can book a videoconference call with the National Baseball Hall of Fame.[1]

Use your math skills and do virtual visits of other baseball stadiums and then compare the difference in distance of the stadiums, the seating capacity, and other stadium statistics.

Holocaust Remembrance Day

(Common Core State Standards: RI.1, RI.3, RI.6, RL.1, RL.6, RL.7, W.2, W.5, W.6, W.7, SL) (ISTE Standards for Students: 2, 3, 5, 6) (ISTE Standards for Teachers: 1, 2, 3, 4)

If possible, host a Skype call or a Google Hangout with a Holocaust survivor or have them come to your school to have them tell their story and even, with their permission, record the session to save as oral history. Prepare your students with lessons on the Holocaust and have them think of pertinent questions for the interview. If you are unable to contact an actual Holocaust survivor, connect with the staff at the Holocaust Survivors and Victims Resource Center at the United States Holocaust Memorial Museum to ask them questions your students have researched.

Visit Yad Vashem's Holocaust History Museum virtually.[2] Yad Vashem is located in Israel and is the World Center for Holocaust Research, Education, Documentation, and Commemoration. This is another easy way in which to have your students learn about a historic event. Students can then write blog posts about what they have learned from their experience. Upper elementary and middle school students can read *Anne Frank: Diary of a Young Girl*, *The Boy in the Striped Pyjamas* by John Boyne, *Number the Stars* by Lois Lowry, *The Book Thief* by Markus Zusak, or *Night* by Elie Wiesel. *The Boy in the Striped Pyjamas* is also a movie, which can be viewed after the book is read. Then students can discuss these books and movies using

Google Classroom, Edmodo, VoiceThread, and other forms of social media for connecting students.

Earth Day—Groceries Project*

(Common Core State Standards: RI, W, SL, MD.4, MD.9) (Next Generation Science Standards: ESS2, ESS3) (ISTE Standards for Students: 1, 2, 3, 4, 5, 6) (ISTE Standards for Teachers: 1, 2, 3, 4)

Earth Day, April 22, is the opportunity to focus on our environment and how to improve it. Have your students come up with some ways to prevent waste or clean up the school or community. Simple things like recycling materials can go a long way toward preserving the environment. A great place to bring items for recycling and turn them into useful items is through a **Makerspace**, which are popping up in libraries and schools around the world. Work with the school administrators, custodial staff, and other staff members on ways to be more environmentally responsible within the school community. Also include the parents of your students in discussions of environmental issues.

One Earth Day project Paula has done allows her students to collaborate within their own community. The Earth Day Groceries Project has you get brown paper bags from your local grocery store and decorate them with Earth Day art and messages.[3]

At the beginning of April, Paula contacts a local grocery store and arranges to pick up a bundle of their brown paper bags. The students do math calculations to figure out how many bags they need to decorate a day in order to have all 400 bags completed before Earth Day. Her students than decorate the bags with Earth-friendly messages and artwork. The bags are returned to the store a few days before April 22, which is Earth Day. The students love seeing their bags going out into their greater community. We have turned this collaboration into another math lesson by figuring out how many trees are used to produce the brown bags for the grocery store each year. We also compare and contrast paper bags to plastic bags, and this year we will be adding reusable grocery bags to the mix. Check out Paula's YouTube video about her Earth Day Groceries Project (www.youtube.com/watch?v=fv0JRv5ZPQI).

Another idea is for students to do short research projects about environmental heroes. Paula created an Environmental Heroes **WebQuest** that can help get you started.[4] The next step to make this a collaborative project is to find other classes to videoconference with and share your research projects.

Arbor Day

(Common Core State Standards: RI.6, W.7, W.9, MD.4, MD.9) (Next Generation Science Standards: ESS2, ESS3) (ISTE Standards for Students: 2, 4, 5, 6) (ISTE Standards for Teachers: 1, 2, 3, 4)

Arbor Day, observed on the last Friday in April, is a holiday to get people to plant or care for trees. Share with another class that you connect with about your state tree and the different types of trees in your area. Discuss the similarities and differences of the trees in each class's region. Determine what effects the location or climate has on the type of trees in their locations. Set up a competition with another class, which could include showing pictures and playing "Name that Tree." Have students do research to come up with three trivia questions.

May Projects

National Inventors Month

(Common Core State Standards: RI.6, W.7, SL, MD.4, MD.9) (Next Generation Science Standards: PS2, PS3, PS4, ETS) (ISTE Standards for Students: 1, 2, 3, 4, 5, 6) (ISTE Standards for Teachers: 1, 2, 3, 4)

With makerspace being so popular in today's educational world, what better way to celebrate National Inventors Month than to talk with inventors and then let students become their own inventors. Makerspace is an area where students get to become the inventor. Take students on a Virtual Field Trip to the Smithsonian Institute. Have your students share their creations with other classes or have a Makerspace competition.

A great article to read with students is "May Is National Inventors Month."[5] Students can research different inventors and share the inventions they create themselves.

10-Day Passion Challenge and Identity Day*

(Common Core State Standards: W, SL) (ISTE Standards for Students: 2, 3, 4, 5) (ISTE Standards for Teachers: 1, 2, 3, 4)

Have you heard of Identity Day, #GeniusHour, 20%time, or Passion Learning? Many teachers have found a way to incorporate the time in their weekly schedule to allow students to pursue their passions. Usually an hour a week is set aside when the students can spend time directing their own learning about a topic they are passionate about.

Several of our PLN members wanted to do something like this with their students but could not find the time within their regular teaching schedule to do so. Paula decided that during May (her last month of school each year), there would be time available for her students to pursue a passion project for a two-week period. She put together a 10-Day Passion Challenge on a Google Doc and invited other interested teachers to join in with their students. Each participating class joined an Edmodo group, and each day a question was posted that got students thinking about their passion. Within the Edmodo group they could respond to the daily question and to other students' responses by using the @ in front of the student's name (for example, @Eric S.).

At the end of the two weeks, interested classes set a date to connect with each other and hold an Identity Day. During Identity Day the classes connected via Skype or Google Hangouts and shared their passion projects, which came in a variety of formats, such as traditional trifold presentation boards, **Glogsters**, videos, blog posts, and more.

Cinco de Mayo (5th of May)*

(Common Core State Standards: RI.6, W, SL) (ISTE Standards for Students: 2, 3, 4, 5) (ISTE Standards for Teachers: 1, 2, 3, 4)

This holiday is an opportunity to learn about other cultures. Have your students find out more about the history of Cinco de Mayo. Encourage them to create projects to illustrate **cultural responsiveness**. Students can connect with other classes and share their illustrations or try and connect with classes in Mexico and interview students to find out the origins of Cinco de Mayo.

Paula's students were treated to a wonderful performance by Louise Morgan's second graders for Cinco de Mayo. Mrs. Morgan, who teaches in San Antonio, Texas, broadcasted her students' presentation via her **Ustream** channel.

Memorial Day

(Common Core State Standards: RI, W, SL) (ISTE Standards for Students: 2, 3, 5, 6) (ISTE Standards for Teachers: 1, 2, 3, 4)

Celebrated on the last Monday in May, Memorial Day presents the opportunity to interview those who have served in the military to find out the importance of this holiday. Connect with other classes around the world to see what they do to honor those who served and died in battle. Work with veterans' groups to help plant flags in military cemeteries to commemorate those who have fallen.

June Projects

Flag Day

(Common Core State Standards: RI, W, SL) (ISTE Standards for Students: 2, 3, 5, 6) (ISTE Standards for Teachers: 1, 2, 3, 4)

Have a flag recognition competition call with another class in honor of Flag Day (June 14). Show the flag of each country around the world and give some hints as to its location. The class that comes up with the most correct country flags will be declared the winner. Share with the other class the countries of the world that the students and staff of the school represent. Work together with your students to develop a flag for your class.

Graduation—End of School

(Common Core State Standards: W, SL) (ISTE Standards for Students: 2, 5, 6) (ISTE Standards for Teachers: 1, 2, 3, 4)

Depending on when your school starts, graduation and the end of school before summer vacation will occur at different times. Connecting with other schools to compare graduation and end-of-school routines would be a wonderful year-end project. Holding a virtual debate about a "hot topic" related to graduation or end-of-year customs is another engaging way to connect and collaborate. Have your current students compose letters for your incoming students, to include words of wisdom, bits of advice, or descriptions of their favorite activities from their school year.

Summer Projects

(ISTE Standards for Teachers: 1, 2, 3, 4, 5)

Summer is a chance for educators to recharge their batteries and plan ahead for the coming school year. It is also a time to reflect on the activities that took place the previous school year and on ways to improve and expand on them. Analyze each connection you had your students make. Review the exit slips of learning your students created after taking part in the Mystery Location Calls. Shore up the weak points and try to come up with new ways to expand your students' learning outside the walls of your classroom. Start preparing more strategies to engage your students in connecting with others.

With more free time available during school vacations, attending conferences, **edcamps**, or **webinars** gives you the opportunity to connect with other educators. Not only can teachers gain ideas, but these can also lead to possible class calls and collaboration. Making connections and building a viable PLN will make it easier to find other classes all around the world with which to share learning adventures. Twitter brought this group of authors together, and we feel it is a great vehicle to use to build your own personal learning network and help you connect your students to collaborations around the world. However, do not neglect other ways to expand your network. Reach out to others on Facebook, LinkedIn, Google+, and other forms of social media.

Teaching summer school also gives you additional chances to connect students to experts and other classes. Try out some new ideas and seek suggestions from the students on ways they would like to connect with other students across the world. Put these ideas in a Google Doc and let other educators, students, and parents give their input.

Summer Learning

Before school ends, have your students work in groups to determine different ways that they can keep learning during the summer. Each group should develop a menu of activities. Have the children plan field trips to interesting places in their community or city. Students have to plan the trip by determining how to get to the place, the costs associated with it, refreshments, and learning outcomes.

Summer Reading

Many public libraries have summer reading programs. Check to see if your local library has such a program and have your students help get the word out about it to their peers. Allow students to come up with their own suggested list of reading materials (books, magazines) they recommend. They can create such lists on their tech devices and can use **QR codes** to show their ratings and comments on books.

If you had your students on Edmodo during the school year, you may want to set up a summer reading group within Edmodo, as was done by several teachers we know. Not only can your students join, but you can share the code with other classes you have connected with during the school year, and have them join in the summer reading fun too! We have found that the students love staying connected to each other during the summer. The teachers can post book reviews and discussion questions for virtual book clubs, and students can write reviews of books they read over the summer.

Resources

April Fools' Day: www.cybraryman.com/april.html
Arbor Day: www.cybraryman.com/plants.html
Autism: www.cybraryman.com/autism.html
Baseball: www.cybraryman.com/baseball.html
Cinco de Mayo: www.cybraryman.com/cincodemayo.html
Coping Strategies: www.cybraryman.com/coping.html
Earth Day: www.cybraryman.com/environment.html
End of School Year and Graduation: www.cybraryman.com/endofschool.html
Exit Slips: www.cybraryman.com/exitslips.html
Father's Day: www.cybraryman.com/fathersday.html
Flag Day: www.cybraryman.com/flagday.html
Holocaust: www.cybraryman.com/holocaust.html
Humor: www.cybraryman.com/humor.html
Inventors: www.cybraryman.com/scientists.html
Learning and Baseball: www.cybraryman.com/baseballlearning.html

Makerspaces: www.cybraryman.com/makerspaces.html
Memorial Day: www.cybraryman.com/memorialday.html
Mother's Day: www.cybraryman.com/mothersday.html
Passion-Based Learning: www.cybraryman.com/passionbasedlearning.html
Standardized Testing: www.cybraryman.com/standardizedtests.html
Summer: www.cybraryman.com/summer.html
Summer Learning: www.cybraryman.com/summerlearning.html
Summer Reading: www.cybraryman.com/summerreading.html
Summer School: www.cybraryman.com/summerschool.html
Teaching the Holocaust: www.npr.org/blogs/ed/2015/02/20/387654149/teaching-the-holocaust-new-approaches-for-a-new-generation

Next Chapter

In Chapter 7 we will explore ways to go on Virtual Field Trips. We will also take a look at a few of the adventures that we have done. This chapter will explore ways to find other Virtual Field Trips.

Notes

1. www.baseballhall.org/education/distance-learning.
2. www.yadvashem.org/yv/en/museum/virtual_tour.asp.
3. www.earthdaybags.org.
4. www.sites.google.com/site/environmentalheroesquest/home.
5. www.dogonews.com/2013/5/6/may-is-national-inventors-month.

7

Virtual Field Trips

In this chapter, we will explore ways to take your students on adventures outside the classroom by taking advantage of virtual field trips (VFTs). There are so many wonderful virtual learning opportunities that can help your students gain knowledge in all subject areas. They can explore and learn about the world without leaving their classroom. Unfortunately, because of cutbacks and the demands of testing, many schools do not provide their students with the opportunity to take actual field trips, so virtual field trips can bring valuable learning to your students. We strongly feel that taking students on actual field trips to explore their community, town, city, or state are great learning experiences. If you are fortunate enough to go on a field trip in person, please Skype or do a Google Hangout with other classes while you are at the site. In this way the students sitting in their classrooms could go along on your adventure too. You can also record the trip and then share it later with other classes.

Jerry used to enjoy taking his classes on trips to historical sites, museums, and office and work sites. One of his all-time favorite trips was to see the Tuskegee Airmen at the Fantasy of Flight Museum in Polk City, Florida, thanks to Dennis Dill (@DennisDill). As a result of tweeting about that event, he found that one of his followers was also in the audience; Diana Rendina (@DianaLRendina) had chaperoned her class from Tampa. It is also a good idea to have your students complete a learning page for either an actual or a virtual field trip. This can be done by using an online survey or a paper form. The main learning features of participating in the trip should be covered. If you are able to take a trip outside your school building, please have your students help plan the trip. They can help determine how you will get to the site and costs involved; also have them prepare some pre-trip information about the place you are visiting.

Most VFTs have lesson plans and standards correlations built in. Many different Common Core State Standards could apply, depending upon the project. Here are a few suggested ones: *(Common Core State Standards RI, W, SL) (Next Generation Science Standards would also tie in depending on the virtual tour you are taking) (ISTE Standards for Students: 2, 3, 4, 5, 6) (ISTE Standards for Teachers: 1, 2, 3, 4, 5, 6).*

Examples of Successful Virtual Field Trips

The following are successful virtual field projects that have or are still taking place. We are including them to give you an idea of what has worked.

Discovery Education and the Good Egg Project

For the past four years, Discovery Education has partnered with the Good Egg Project to host a VFT to a different egg farm in the United States each spring. Teachers can sign up to take part in the VFT and their students can post questions prior to the actual trip. On the designated date and time, students from around the United States tune in and are taken around the host farm's facilities and are given plenty of information about eggs and egg production. Students learn how eggs get from the farm to their table. The Good Egg Project's Education Station maintains an archive of all of the Good Egg Virtual Field Trips.[1] Check out Discovery Education in March to sign up for this exciting event.

Decorah Eagle Cam

In the winter of 2011, Paula learned about the Decorah Eagle cam[2] from Nancy Carroll's blog post "Teachable Moment—Watch Live—Iowa Eagles."[3] The next day Paula had her students viewing the live stream. The excitement generated by watching this live feed spread throughout our building and community, and soon everyone was talking about it. I wrote about paying it forward on my blog.[4] We checked on the eagles daily and were thrilled to witness the hatching of the eggs. We were sad when the last eaglet was old enough to fledge the nest. However, each year starting in February, the Decorah eagles become a part of our classroom and we share things we observe with others during video calls.

Arctic Adaptations: Tundra Connections Webcast with DEN—November 2012

As a member of the DEN (Discovery Educator Network), Paula learns about virtual field trips that Discovery Education hosts through their weekly email updates. When she saw the opportunity to visit the Arctic tundra and learn more about polar bears, she shared the information with her PLN on Twitter. Both Billy's class and Paula's class took part in this VFT: Arctic Adaptations: Tundra Connections Webcast with DEN on YouTube.[5]

Take the journey with us as we explore how Billy, who teaches in New Jersey, took a class from Massachusetts on a virtual tour of the Statue of Liberty, Ellis Island, and the Intrepid Air and Space Museum.

In the spring of 2012, Billy started to experiment with going beyond the Mystery Location Call. The fourth-grade students at Beatrice Gilmore Elementary School in New Jersey were headed to Ellis Island and the Statue of Liberty for their school field trip. Nancy Carroll in Massachusetts and Billy had been in contact and playing with ideas of how to connect beyond the Mystery Location Call. Back then they were just using Skype. In Chapter 5 we learned one way in which Nancy and Billy took their Mystery Location Call further by learning about Indianapolis and had their fun with Super Bowl XLVI. Now you might be saying to yourself, well that is a pretty fun way of expanding the Mystery Location Call, but Nancy and Billy took it a step farther.

Nancy's class was studying Ellis Island and just happened to finish the unit. Prior to the field trip Billy and Nancy discussed a possible Skype call during the field trip depending on connectivity. Billy attempted to make a Skype call and was able to get through to bring Ellis Island virtually to Nancy's class in Massachusetts. This call lasted about 15–20 minutes through Billy's cell phone. The students in Massachusetts were able to see the different places at Ellis Island as Billy ran around showing them the Great Hall, the Registry Room, the Statue of Liberty, and the American Immigrant Wall of Honor. The students also were able to see the building of the "Freedom Tower" as it is visible from Ellis Island.

Scholastic offers a great interactive tour of Ellis Island as well if you cannot make the trip in person or don't have a class with which to connect.[6] The National Park Service also offers a virtual field trip to Ellis Island, part of Statue of Liberty National Monument.[7] If you are looking for some information about the history of Ellis Island, make sure to visit "Ellis Island—Facts & Summary" on History.com and Jerry's Cybraryman site.[8]

In the spring of 2013, Billy again took Nancy's class on a VFT with his fourth-grade class. This year the students at Beatrice Gilmore Elementary School visited the Intrepid Air and Space Museum for a guided tour. The students in Massachusetts were able to learn about the Intrepid along with

Figure 7.1 View of the Freedom Tower being constructed.

Figure 7.2 View of Ellis Island from the boat.

the students in New Jersey. They were even able to look up pictures on the Internet about the planes the guide was talking about.

Connected Classrooms: Explore the Tundra with Polar Bears International and Google Street View

Who doesn't love polar bears? This was a collaborative effort between the Google Maps team and Polar Bears International.[9] It took place in Churchill, Manitoba, one of the world's best places to see polar bears. Lots of Google Street View imagery was shared, the two classes that were a part of the actual Hangout asked great questions, and others learned a lot from just viewing this virtual field trip via Google On Air.

Lab Tour at Florida International University

In May 2014, Paula's class took part in a virtual field trip hosted by EarthEcho International to the Florida International University's lab via Google On Air. They learned about the work scientists are doing there to help save endangered ocean animals. Her students were thrilled when a question they submitted was answered by scientist Nicholas, who was giving the tour.[10]

Maker Camp: Blasting Off with Buzz Aldrin and NASA

This particular VFT took place during July 2014. While Paula was enjoying her summer vacation, she was so excited to have a chance to "hang out" with Buzz Aldrin that she shared the information with her previous students through their Edmodo group. She also shared the information with parents of both previous and incoming students by posting the information and link to this event through various social media sites such as Facebook and Twitter. Several of her students did attend this Google On Air Event[11]

Dennis Dill in Florida (@DennisDill) Connects His Students with South Africa

Dennis Dill describes his collaborative experience:

> By definition collaboration is the action of working with someone to produce or create something and it seems as though it has become an education buzzword embraced by many to illustrate how we are assisting kids into becoming college and career ready, but is this the only way to view this action?
>
> I had the opportunity to connect with George Hasani, a Principal at a K-12 school in South Africa when he visited my school in the United States with a group of his students. After a conversation about

his students' and staff's needs and wants we saw an opportunity to assist. We wanted to help him with professional development for his staff and create an enhanced learning environment for his students. The enhancement is not coming in the form of teachers from the United States teaching them, but through students in the United States connecting and assisting in their learning . . . Collaboration with a Purpose.

Collaboration with a Purpose views collaboration not as just completing a project, but rather making a difference. This is a bit different than working with people and planting some trees and making a difference in the environment, which is a great project, but this collaboration is making a tangible difference in a person's life. In this case, my students will be working with students in South Africa and there will be the requisite cultural exchange, which will benefit both parties, but the change shift happens when this interaction turns into conversational English tutoring. Yes, there will be collaborative projects, but the outcomes or goals of the project are different for each student. From the South African perspective, it is to learn English, Math, and Science through interacting with American students, but from the American perspective each South African student is a collaborative project.

We have a couple of different ways we connect. We try to connect regularly via Skype, but with the seven hour time difference and different school schedules it makes it challenging.

Student-Created Virtual Field Trips

With the technology tools available today, have your students create their own virtual field trips to historical sites or interesting things in your community, town, or city. You can even create one of your school (make sure if you include any pictures of students that you have signed permission forms). You can also develop a VFT of your school to share and compare with other classes. Divide the class up for this project and assign students jobs as in the Mystery Location Call.

Some suggested jobs:

Project manager oversees the entire operation and ensures all students are working on their jobs.
Site selectors choose interesting places in the community, town, or city to do this project.

Researchers gather interesting material on the site.

Script writers choose the wording that will be used in the production.

Scenery locators select interesting places to film the production.

Videographers are the team of students who will capture the trip on film.

Tech map coordinators make use of Google Maps and Google Earth to create visuals (see the next section, "Google Maps and Virtual Field Trips").

Hosts are on air and will introduce the project and take us through it from beginning to end.

Sound and visual engineers do checks to make sure the quality of the audio is clear and good.

Evaluators view the project before it is released and make suggestions to improve the project.

Once the project is complete, you can then share it with classes that you have connected with in other states or countries.

Google Maps and Virtual Field Trips

Google Maps is a great way to explore different locations. "Google Maps for Education provides resources to help teachers and students explore, create, and collaborate with mapping tools. Students who are taught geography are better equipped to understand how human and physical systems interact and to make informed decisions based on that knowledge."[12] Visit the Liwa Desert, North East through Google Camel View.[13] Google also offers some fantastic street views of famous locations from around the world.[14] We suggest downloading Google Earth to explore other lands as well.

Are you exploring or studying the oceans? Then this a must visit: Google Maps' Street View, Oceans offers an interactive guide through the underwater world of the oceans.[15]

If you are learning about different art museums, make sure you visit the website of the Google Cultural Institute and take tours of all the different art museums from around the world.[16]

Google has a new product called Tour Builder, which is part of Build with Chrome. "Tour Builder is a new way to show people the places you've visited and the experiences you had along the way using Google Earth. It lets you pick the locations right on the map, add in photos, text, and video, and then share your creation."[17] Although students will enjoy viewing tours built by others, they will really be engaged when they create their own story. Here is a YouTube video tutorial to help you get started: "Google Earth Tour Builder HowTo."[18]

Google Lit Trips allows a reader to integrate the technology of Google Earth with places visited by characters in a novel.[19] The Google Lit Trip site has files you download and run in Google Earth, which contain placemarks of places cited in that particular book. The placemarks can also contain supplementary material, including photos, videos, discussion questions, and links to other sites that allow the reader to "get into the book." You can also build your own Google Lit Trip and share it with others. Image having your class collaborate with one or more classes to create a Google Lit Trip based on a novel read by all.

Connected Classrooms: Google+ Community Virtual Field Trips

If you like to participate in VFTs, we suggest joining the Google+ Community Virtual Field Trips. By accessing this link (http://connectedclassrooms. withgoogle.com/), you can learn about the community, how to use Google Hangouts and Google On Air, and how to join the community. Many of the past virtual field trips are archived at this link so that you can view them with your students.

Historical Sites

Thanks to the available technology today, you can take your class on virtual field trips to places you are studying from history. For instance, visit the Battle of Gettysburg through Virtual Gettysburg: The Ultimate Battlefield Tour for Windows and Macintosh.[20]

Resources

Bringing Social Studies to Life: www.teachhub.com/bringing-social-studies-life
Field Trips: www.cybraryman.com/fieldtrips.html
Google: www.cybraryman.com/google.html
North America Virtual Field Trips: www.discoveryeducation.com/northamerica/event.cfm
Virtual Tours and Fieldtrips: www.theteachersguide.com/virtualtours.html#Museums
Explore Plimoth Plantation: www.plimoth.org/learn

Kids as Tour Guides: Integrating Student-Created Media into History Class: www.edsurge.com/n/2015-02-20-kids-as-tour-guides-integrating-student-created-media-into-history-class

Kiker Symbaloo: www.sites.google.com/site/kikerlearning/google-dashboard

This Land Is Your Land: www.oiadaintl.org/

Notes

1. http://educationstation.discoveryeducation.com/field-trips.
2. Decorah eagles, Ustream.TV, www.ustream.tv/decoraheagles.
3. www.teachingiselementary.blogspot.com/2011/04/teachable-moment.html.
4. A teachable moment—pay it forward, Ms. Naugle's Classroom Blog, www.pnaugle.blogspot.com/2011/04/teachable-moment-pay-it-forward.html.
5. www.youtube.com/watch?v=iiP_9yCDifY.
6. Ellis Island interactive tour with facts, pictures, video, Scholastic.com, www.teacher.scholastic.com/activities/immigration/tour/.
7. www.nps.gov/elis/learn/education/learning/scholastic-virtual-field-trip.htm.
8. www.history.com/topics/ellis-island; www.cybraryman.com/immigration.html
9. https://plus.google.com/u/0/events/ccf8j1o7l92dkr43826tai21ov8.
10. Virtual Field Trip: Lab tour at Florida International University, Google+, https://plus.google.com/u/0/events/cb0tio3uqes71qjg51vai7qrtug (at 38:51).
11. Maker Camp: Blasting off with Buzz Aldrin and NASA, Google+, https://plus.google.com/events/cm2rsvo58t3scdtb2b622aidsb8.
12. Education, Google Maps, www.maps.google.com/help/maps/education/.
13. www.goo.gl/x37vuf.
14. www.google.com/maps/views/u/0/home?gl=us.
15. www.google.com/maps/views/u/0/streetview/oceans?gl=us.
16. www.google.com/culturalinstitute/u/0/project/art-project.
17. https://tourbuilder.withgoogle.com/about/faq.
18. www.youtube.com/watch?v=Z2XyCA90nyU.
19. www.googlelittrips.com/GoogleLit/Home.html.
20. www.virtualgettysburg.com.

8

Stories from Our PLN about Connecting Globally

The authors have taken you step-by step through a Mystery Location Call in Chapter 2, "The Practical Guide to a Mystery Location Call." They have gone through the seasons of the year with different projects and ideas that you can do with your classroom and ways to collaborate with other classes. Now they are going to take you on firsthand adventures through their personal learning network and share their stories about how they connected globally. You will be introduced to teachers from around the world sharing their own stories from their classrooms about how they connected with others. The authors will also give some takeaways from each of these stories.

Nancy Carroll's Story: Global Connections

Location: Massachusetts
Twitter Handle: @ncarroll24

You never know where your Global Connections will take you and your class! One of my first Mystery Skype calls was with Billy Krakower's 4th grade class in New Jersey. Right away our classes hit it off, so Billy and I knew we had to plan some other connections.

Our classes connected a second time as both our area football teams were heading to Indiana to face each other in Super Bowl XLVI. We Skyped with each other and one class shared information about Indiana while the other class shared facts about the Stadium.

It just so happened that Billy's class was traveling to nearby Ellis Island for a field trip right around the time my students were exploring the topic of Immigration and Ellis Island from further away Massachusetts. Billy mentioned to me that he would "Skype" our class using his cell phone while he was there. Pretty much it worked like a charm (although the weather wasn't so great). My students were not only able to see the Statue of Liberty but were able to experience it vicariously through their 4th grade counterparts. Seeing Ellis Island's Grand Hall and hearing the commotion of visitors caused an audible gasp in my classroom as the students recognized the area they had only seen in pictures.

While on Twitter one evening I mentioned to a fellow fourth grade teacher that my class was traveling to Plimoth Plantation in Plymouth, MA to learn more about the Pilgrims and Wampanoag Indians.

She tweeted back: "Jealous!"

As she is located in Indiana it made me sad to think that she and her class would never, in all likelihood, get to experience this amazing "living" museum. Inspired by Billy Krakower's idea of taking us along via Skype, that's when my "Shared Field Trip" using Edmodo was born!

As I was new Edmodo user at the time I had been looking for ways to seamlessly incorporate it into my daily lessons. Being able to connect and collaborate on projects with classrooms around the globe made this a valuable real world tool. Knowing that many of my Twitter PLN also use Edmodo made me think that this would be an effective way to share our trip.

How It Worked

Created an Edmodo Group and Tweeted the "request to join" URL a day or two before the trip

Students/Classes joined the Plimoth Plantation Field Trip Group

Links to set prior knowledge were shared to the Group

Groups brainstormed and asked questions about Pilgrims/ Wampanoags

2 iPads were utilized on the field trip to retrieve/respond to the groups' inquiries

Further responses were made upon our return to our classroom

Helpful Hints

Group code or "request to join" URL should be sent out well in advance (a week or more)

Questions should be made known before leaving for the trip

Upload Video & audio links from the trip

Decide ahead if the "shared field trip" will be in "real time"
Check for Wifi connections before arrival
Try to use more than one device

Benefits

Motivating for students
Makes trip even more interactive
Gives students greater purpose
Many students/groups benefit from shared knowledge
Connecting and Collaborating Globally

My students were more motivated knowing their counterparts in the Edmodo group wanted information. It became important for them to inquire for the "group" as they realized this was a way to help the students in the far away classes. Each one of my students wanted to be able to respond and be a part of the learning. I heard from the other teachers in the Edmodo group that their students were just as excited to receive answers from us, thereby extending the learning for all.

(In case you were wondering—Mr. Krakower's class also came along. Using my smartphone and Skype, the class wandered in and out of the Plimoth Village (in real-time) and had several opportunities to listen to the Pilgrims as they spoke with my students. Questions from the New Jersey students were relayed to the Pilgrims via my students (as folks in the 1620's would never have understood a smartphone, never mind Skype!).

Shared field trips provide a wonderful opportunity for students to connect globally! The possibilities are endless.

Takeaways from Nancy's Story

The use of Edmodo for prior knowledge is a great way to start a connection with other classrooms. Edmodo is a free tool for teachers and very easy to use. You can create groups that are closed to the public, and the teacher has full control over everything that gets posted.

The use of an iPad or cell phone and the Edmodo free app to connect during a Virtual Field Trip is important.

Jennifer Regruth's Story: Making Global Connections

Location: Indiana
Twitter Handle: @jennregruth

I would like to say right away that Twitter, hands down, has been the driving force in my professional life the last four years. I decided to sign up for Twitter and was completely blown away by its educational content and collaborative opportunities. I interacted with professors, teachers, tech directors, coding developers . . . and all kinds of people not in education—the list is endless. It was here I found my "Birds of a Feather" friends, Billy Krakower, Jerry Blumengarten, Paula Naugle, Nancy Carroll, Dan Curio, Jessica Bamberger, and Kim Powell. I jumped at the chance to join their weekly GHO to discuss all types of topics. I cannot express how joining up with these folks and the ones I met on Twitter has changed my life and teaching. In this crazy world of education, I felt centered, supported and inspired by my Twitter PLN (Professional Learning Network).

Last year at ISTE in Atlanta (my first) I was finally able to meet most of this incredible group in person. After all we had shared, advised, collaborated on, and talked about, I finally got to bear hug them and thank them for being such an important part of my teaching and personal lives.

One great way the kids and I made connections around the globe was in collaboration with my Twitter friend, Arin Kress (@arinkress). I say Twitter friend, because although we have collaborated on many projects, we have never met in person. We met on Twitter a few years ago, found many educational similarities, and started sharing. We decided to do a "Skype Around the World" project by sharing contacts, formulating questions, and sharing what we [were] learning. When the project was such a big hit with the kids, we decided to then include parents and "Skype Around the World in 2 Hours." It was an evening event, she and her class in Ohio, and me with mine in Indiana, alternating calls between us. What a success! Students and parents met folks from Australia, Holland, Uganda, Canada, Brazil, Antarctica, and Japan . . . all in two hours. We took notes on main exports, population, cuisine, and lifestyles. With the amazing world of technology and Skype, and a great collaborative partner, we showed parents and students the power of collaboration.

Another way our class is able to connect globally is through a program called Classroom Champions. After applying and being accepted, our class was paired for the year with Olympic athletes Meryl Davis and Charlie White. We were able to wish them luck for the 2014 Olympics during our first live GHO with them, ask questions and get to know them.

During the Olympics, we were able to connect with a gold medal winner in bobsledding live from the athlete village in Sochi, Russia! He talked to us about the village for the athletes, competition, food in the cafeteria, and what an honor it is to compete for the USA. A few days later, we watched live as Meryl and Charlie won their gold medals in ice dancing! We were so proud! Then in early May, we had our second live chat with them! We made signs and chanted, "USA!" Then they showed us their gold medals and we were able to ask questions about their experience.

Takeaways from Jennifer's Story

Being a connected educator on Twitter leads to wonderful learning opportunities for my students. Finding like-minded educators helps me feel centered, supported, and inspired. I am able to bring experts into my classroom and expand my students' background knowledge on many topics.

Diana L. Rendina's Story: Connecting Students to the World in Makerspaces

> Location: Florida
> Twitter Handle: @DianaLRendina

When we first started our makerspace in our library at Stewart Middle Magnet School in Tampa, Florida, the focus was only on students within our school. As my students continued to make amazing projects, I knew that we needed to find ways to share these projects with the world. We created social media accounts on Twitter, Instagram and Vine and started to share projects on these accounts regularly. My students began to get excited as I told them of the positive feedback on their projects. While social media was a great way to put my students' works out there, I knew that there had to be more that I could do to help them share their creations with the world and connect with other makers.

I don't remember exactly when the first conversation happened, but somewhere through chatting on Twitter, Colleen Graves, teacher-librarian at Lamar Middle School in Lamar, Texas, and I decided that it would be awesome to connect our Maker kids. I have an afterschool STEAM club that meets on Mondays at the same time as her Maker Mondays group, even though we're in different time zones. When our groups "met" for the first time through Skype, my students were so excited to share projects they were working on. They proudly shared their creations like a remote controlled littleBits car and a cardboard basketball shooter arcade game. They were so happy to find other kids who loved to create things like they did.

After talking with both of our groups after that first meet-up, Colleen and I began a joint-design challenge project. My STEAM club and her Maker Mondays group began working on the Catapult Challenge, where our students had to design and build a working catapult out of any material of their choosing. The challenge quickly turned into "build-something-that-flings-something-across-the-room" as students at both designed crossbows, ballistas and even trebuchets!

At the end of the challenge, we met up in a Google Hangout and shared our projects. Colleen's students had made some amazing giant catapults capable of flinging multiple ketchup packets at once. My kids proudly showed off their creations and were ecstatic that they worked. They happily conversed with the students in Texas about how each group came up with their design, what problems they encountered, and how they solved them. They didn't realize it, but they were describing and discussing 21st century skills like design-thinking, collaboration, and problem solving.

We've decided to continue to have regular design challenges with Lamar throughout the year. It's become an amazing catalyst for my students' projects. Knowing that students in Lamar, Texas will be seeing their projects makes them want to do their very best. Many of my students have never left the state of Florida. By meeting with Lamar virtually on a regular basis, these students are now able to expand their horizons farther than ever before.

Takeaways from Diana's Story

Oftentimes, what starts out as a class or school-wide project ends up being shared with students in other schools. Time zone constraints can be overcome when the enthusiasm for a project takes hold of the participants. Once an initial contact has been made it can lead to other collaborative undertakings and challenges.

Kevin Jarrett's Story: Pedagogical Serendipity (or, How Twitter Saved My Kindergarten Lesson)[1]

Location: New Jersey
Twitter Handle: @kjarrett

Planning lessons is hard.

I teach in a K-4 computer lab. 25 classes, five classes a day, each class once a week, 42 minutes each. Like most people who teach in a lab, I'm constantly on the lookout for great lesson material, particularly ideas that tie into what the kids are learning in their regular classrooms.

So I was thrilled when my Kindergarten teachers took the time to share some lesson/project ideas they found in our Language Arts series. They provided me a photocopied list of monthly "Culminating Performance

Tasks" (CPTs) with timing suggestions ("sometime in December," etc.) and I was set!

Or so I thought.

So, our Kindergarteners were currently learning about farms. This particular month's CPT suggested the students "research farms on the Internet." Huh, what? Kindergarteners? Many of whom are non-readers? Doing Internet research? On their own? Not happening!

I was back to the drawing board.

In the not too distant past, my options would have involved emailing friends and some frantic but focused Google searches in pursuit of similar lesson plans and resources like the "4-H Virtual Farm." (That site is good, but is still not suitable for non-readers to navigate without assistance.)

But, this is 2009—educators like me now have something better. *Twitter!*

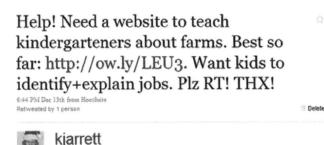

Help! Need a website to teach kindergarteners about farms. Best so far: http://ow.ly/LEU3. Want kids to identify+explain jobs. Plz RT! THX!

6:44 PM Dec 13th from HootSuite
Retweeted by 1 person   Delete

kjarrett
Kevin Jarrett

A vibrant conversation ensued, involving several members of my PLN, including my friend and colleague Gary Stager.[2] He seized the opportunity to do what he does best—challenge our assumptions, forcing us to think differently about the learning and our approach.

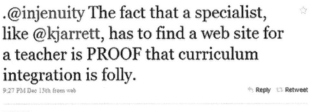

.@injenuity The fact that a specialist, like @kjarrett, has to find a web site for a teacher is PROOF that curriculum integration is folly.

9:27 PM Dec 13th from web   Reply Retweet

garystager

The discussion continued without me—I had to turn in for the night—but along the way I got connected to Brenda Sherry.

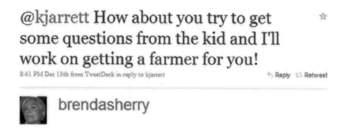

@kjarrett How about you try to get some questions from the kid and I'll work on getting a farmer for you!

8:41 PM Dec 13th from TweetDeck in reply to kjarrett   ↩ Reply ⇅ Retweet

brendasherry

Her neighbor, a dairy farmer, had just delivered over 100 baby calves. I also met Penny Lindballe, the teacher wife of a grain farmer. We were on our way!

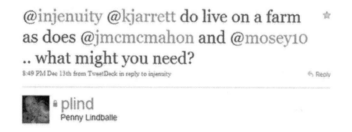

@injenuity @kjarrett do live on a farm as does @jmcmcmahon and @mosey10 .. what might you need?

8:49 PM Dec 13th from TweetDeck in reply to injenuity   ↩ Reply

plind
Penny Lindballe

At this point, I had (at least) two willing teachers ready to connect my students with real farms and farm life. My first thought was Skype, but with five lessons to deliver on five different days, it didn't seem feasible. I needed an approach that was repeatable, reusable, flexible, and respectful of the time these volunteers were able to offer. Logistics threatened to sink my grandiose plan to connect my class and students to the outside world in a meaningful, powerful, authentic way.

Then, Penny suggested getting her family to contribute to a VoiceThread for our class and it hit me—VoiceThread was the answer! It would give us the ability to "converse" asynchronously, using text, audio and video. VoiceThread's navigation is dead simple; I know my kindergarten students can easily make their way through material presented that way. VoiceThread's asynchronous nature means that Brenda, Penny and anyone else we bring into the mix can contribute ideas easily and at their own convenience. Thank you Penny!

All we needed were questions from the students. Another member of my personal learning network (PLN) whose tweet I cannot find (so sorry!) suggested I use photos to spark a conversation among the kids. So, I headed over to Flickr and created this gallery of farm pics. So far, it's been working GREAT! The students are really reacting to the photos. By the end of this week, all my students will have had the chance to ask questions (which I captured using my digital voice recorder). I will insert the questions into the VoiceThread I created for Brenda, Penny and the others to see and use.[3]

My Canadian farmer friends had the entire last week of December to contribute text, audio and video responses to my students' questions. When we returned to school in January, students spent the beginning of my computer lab class reviewing the VoiceThread. Imagine—learning about farms directly from farmers themselves, in their own words, from the comfort of our classrooms! Short of visiting an actual farm, what could be more fun? The students then used Tux Paint to create an image explaining what they learned about farms, including something involving (a) farm animals, (b) farm people, and (c) farm crops.

How cool was this? Penny, Brenda, and I loved how this collaborative project came together![4]

Yes, planning lessons is hard.

But when you engage a global PLN filled with creative, thoughtful and fun-loving lifelong learners in the process, amazing things can happen!

Takeaways from Kevin's Story

Serendipitous moments often occur for connected educators thanks to social media venues. Kevin reaching out on Twitter helped create a lesson that became so much more than just another lesson about farms. He was able to take his students on a trip and really learn about farms just by reaching out to his PLN. When videoconferencing was not a viable option, an asynchronous tool like VoiceThread can be used instead. It is amazing the connections, resources, and information you can gain by being a connected educator.

Kim Powell's Story: Global Collaboration

Location: Michigan
Twitter Handle: @kimpowelledtech

How can we learn about the environmental effects of weather in a particular region through collaboration with other classrooms throughout the world?

Global collaboration allows the opportunity to extend our knowledge through personal connections and extensions of others in the environment.

This particular project was created by Billy Krakower and Kim Powell as a part of the **Flat Classroom** Certified Teaching program. The focus of the project was to answer three questions:

What is typical weather in different parts of the world?
How is weather affected by Global Warming?
How does weather impact the way we live?

To learn from one another for this project, each classroom was to create a presentation using choice of tools—ThingLink, Glogster, NewHive, Edcanvas or Smore.

Students will create graphs to represent the weather where they live.
Students will share picture[s] of the weather.
Students will create a VoiceThread in Subgroups to discuss impact of
    Global Warming.

In participating with this project, students will gain an understanding of how weather is different across regions.

Students will work collaboratively to gather and share data with classmates and others using web 2.0 tools.

Students will build a personal learning environment in Edmodo.

Students will obtain and combine information to describe the climate of different regions throughout the world.

The workflow of this project can be broken down as follows:

Project will be introduced the first week in September.
Classroom will join Edmodo and participate in initial handshakes.
The next two weeks will be used to gather data within the groups.
The following week students will create their multimedia project to be
    shared in Edmodo group for all project participants.
A signup sheet will be shared for further collaborations with the
    projects using Skype/Google Hangout.
Collaborations and extensions will take place the first week in
    October.

Building connections is an essential element when working on a global collaborative project. They will have the opportunity to connect in a variety of ways.

Students and teachers will use **Animoto** to create handshakes to introduce themselves into other groups.

Students will be able to view the Animotos in Edmodo.

Classroom will be involved in Edmodo and Wiki.

Students and teachers are expected to connect and share their information on weekly basis.

This project will also allow students to effectively communicate and demonstrate positive digital citizenship skills as they move forward in a 21st Century Learning Environment. Students will share graphs and information found via Google Hangouts or Skype group calling, where they can screenshare the projects they have created.

Takeaways from Kim's Story

Students learning from other students is much more powerful than learning from a book. Having connections to people and places brings learning opportunities that enrich the curriculum. This is such a great way to practice speaking and listening skills.

Todd LaVogue: Global Connection Project

Location: Florida
Twitter Handle: @ToddLaVogue

The students in my eighth grade Innovation Class at Watson B. Duncan Middle School love the global connection projects we have completed as part of our project based learning curriculum. Along with meeting ISTE/NETS standards my students have learned about geography, cultures and human relations.

Our most recent learning activity was with a classroom in Oulu, Finland. We teamed up to research Windows 8 apps made by Corinth, a company from the Czech Republic. Corinth has numerous education apps. Teams were created with students from both countries on each team, focusing on one app per team. The teams "dissected" their selected app and, using multimedia tools, presented their findings to Corinth of what they thought was great and what could be modified, from a student's perspective. Corinth took the information and will use it in the creation of future educational apps. Using virtual collaboration tools like Skype and **Yammer**, the students were able to conquer seven time zones, language and cultural barriers.

Previous projects were created with countries in France, Tunisia, Taiwan and Indonesia. We are currently searching for our next project in a new country.

Takeaways from Todd's Story

This was a wonderful opportunity for students in different countries to connect and to have a say in improving an educational app. More technology companies should listen to their potential student users and consider their ideas about products.

Jessica Bamberger's Story: Classroom Champions

Location: Pennsylvania
Twitter Handle: @MissBamberger

I had the privilege of being chosen to be a part of the project called Classroom Champions. Classroom Champions is an organization that connects teachers with Olympians who are preparing for or competing [in] the Olympic Games. This year our Classroom Champion is Taylor Ritzel. She is an Olympic rower who is preparing to compete in the 2016 Olympic games in Rio de Janeiro, Brazil.

Since September, she has sent us video messages that my students have absolutely loved. She encourages them to practice a positive character trait of the month. Taylor also gives the students challenges to help them learn and grow, physically, emotionally and socially. We had the privilege of connecting with her for a live Skype call where she has answered our questions and helped us refocus on our goals and dreams. Each week, the students in my classroom ask about when we will have "Classroom Champions" time. They look forward to connecting with her and have learned many positive skills from her video calls.

Takeaways from Jessica's Story

Connecting students to real-life athletes who will be representing our country in the Olympics is definitely an uplifting experience for students. The messages that these champions deliver will hopefully inspire students to "go for the gold."

Jessica Bamberger's Story: Antarctic Penguins

Location: Pennsylvania
Twitter Handle: @MissBamberger

Over the past two years, I have been able to connect my class with a penguin expert, known as Jean, in Antarctica. This particular connection came from reading someone else's tweet on Twitter and responding to it. Part of our English Language Arts (ELA) curriculum includes reading informational text about Antarctica. The text talks about glaciers, icebergs, penguins, and other interesting information about living in Antarctica.

I decided that after our week of reading and writing about Antarctica there would be nothing better than to make it come alive, by having a penguin expert who is currently stationed in Antarctica talk to our class via Skype. We spent the week preparing questions and becoming experts ourselves. When the time came we were ready to increase our knowledge even more! We learned some really amazing things on that Skype call! To top off the week and all our learning, our friend Jean, decided to take us down to the rookery and show us the penguins, eggs and chicks! This is a connection that I hope to be able to keep for as long as I am [a] teacher. There is nothing like taking 50 students virtually to Antarctica after they learned about it through reading and writing all week!

Takeaways from Jessica's Story

Making virtual connections after learning about something in print format helps enhance student knowledge. Students being able to visually see what they just studied allows for better retention. The technology available today allows teachers to enhance lessons to a degree that has never been imagined before. Look for ways to connect your students beyond books. Check out sites such as Skype in the Classroom and Discovery Education.

Melissa Butler's Story: Virtual Debate

Location: New Jersey
Twitter Handle: @AngelinaShy

Melissa Butler, the sixth-grade ELA teacher, and Elissa Malespina, the former librarian/media specialist from South Orange Middle School (SOMS) revolutionized their argument writing/debate unit by thinking beyond the four walls of the classroom, by taking risks, and by modernizing a more authentic way of meeting the Common Core State Standards. Melissa and Elissa conjured up this idea in their school of reaching all learners at all levels through the utilization of social media and web 2.0 tools. These game changers have transformed Melissa's classroom into a more student-driven and powerfully engaged culture for teachers and students alike. With their commitment to unlimited opportunities also came their open-mindedness and willingness to become vulnerable with other teachers, with other schools and with other students . . . a journey that *could* have gone terribly wrong.

First came the tweet to a member in their Twitter PLN, Dana Sirotiak, former seventh-grade social studies teacher at the Frank R. Conwell Middle School #4 in Jersey City, New Jersey. Dana was willing to embark on this learning exploration, using her cellular phone as a **hotspot**, because obstacles weren't an option in her mind. Then the vision began, two New Jersey schools versus two Pennsylvania schools. Melissa and Elissa had recently connected with Thomas Murray, the former director of technology for the Quakertown School District and now state and district Digital Learning Director for Alliance for Excellent Education, and asked him if he had a teacher in mind for the debate. He connected us with Shawn Storm, who teaches sixth-grade ELA, all via Twitter, our virtual learning playground. Then came the tweet to Joe Mazza, the principal at Knapp Elementary School in Lansdale, Pennsylvania. Both Melissa and Elissa had recently spoke to his teachers via Google Hangout during an in-service day in reference to the benefits of being a connected educator. Joe asked Gabby Morrison, a sixth-grade ELA teacher, if she was interested in participating in the virtual debate with her students. Now the four official schools were finalized for the virtual debate.

The first Google Hangout session took place for the flipping of the coin to see which state would assume each side of the argument concerning homework. New Jersey won the coin toss and chose the side of pro (homework) and Pennsylvania took the side of con (homework). Then the intense research for the debate launched.

Here is the recording of the coin toss: Debate Introductions, http://youtu.be/l8sDshpR6m4.

After the coin toss, the SOMS teachers set up an Edmodo group, so the two New Jersey schools could communicate and collaborate together prior to the actual debate. This was the primary method that the students used to communicate during the research portion of the unit and also during the actual debate itself both for the teamwork aspect and for the backchanneling. Elissa also created a LiveBinder (password protected) for the two New Jersey schools, where resources could be compiled and stored for **close reading** and research.[5]

The next action would be to satisfy one of the requirements that Melissa set forth for her students: obtaining a live interview with an expert in the field. After conducting immense research one night on the topic, Melissa saw that her Twitter friend Jerry Blumengarten (@cybraryman1) had an entire page on his website devoted to homework (he literally has a page for everything). She tweeted him to see if he could Google Hangout with her students, in order to conduct an official interview concerning the facts around the homework debate. Here is the live interview: Homework Debate Interview, http://youtu.be/i8ka4rnulaU.

The students also reached out to Dr. Harris Cooper, who has done comprehensive research on homework. He could not join the students via Google Hangout, because of scheduling restraints, but he emailed us a link to an article containing a vast amount of research.

The students spent the next week investigating evidence on both sides of the argument, suspending judgment, and extending the counter-argument so the audience feels heard. With debate, writers begin to imagine the counter-arguments for their positions in order to strengthen their own argument. Students were able to think of the evidence against their position and how they might show that the evidence is not telling the full story or is overlooking something else or is not as strong.

Next came the task of obtaining judges for the debate. Melissa preferred to refrain from having judges within the four schools to prevent biased judgment during the debate. For this reason, Melissa and Elissa tweeted out to their PLN and asked them if they would contribute as judges virtually via Google Hangout. They received more than the six virtual judges needed because everyone was eager to explore something new that was happening in the classroom and perhaps bring it back to their own school. Melissa provided a detailed debate rubric, so all judges could determine their decision based on the same criterion.

The debate judges were:

Shannon Miller—a former librarian, author, speaker, and consultant from Iowa;
Will Richardson—author, speaker, and consultant from New Jersey;
Jeff Bradbury—music teacher, speaker, and the man behind the Teachercast website and podcasts from New Jersey;
Sandra Paul—technology director, speaker from New Jersey;

Kyle Calderwood—former adjunct professor and IT director from
    Stockton College, New Jersey;
Jay Eitner—Superintendent of Schools in New Jersey;
Billy Krakower—technology teacher, speaker from New Jersey (he
    watched the video of the debate).

There was also a need for a moderator, so the proceedings were moderated by the South Orange Village president (also known as the mayor), Alex Torpey.

Before school and after school became the norm for all of the students as they prepared extensively for the upcoming virtual debate. Google Docs and Google Hangouts became a part of the virtual classroom on the weekends for both students and teachers, so learning could extend beyond the classroom. The first year of the debate brought giant cue cards to prompt the students during the debate. Then as the past two years have progressed, reflective teaching and learning has resulted in the students becoming true experts in the field, requiring no cue cards, just pure knowledge and speaking and language preparation.

On the day of the debate,

- ◆ All schools and judges are invited into the Google Hangout.
- ◆ The Google Hangout goes live, in order to provide parents the opportunity to become a part of the learning environment from their workplace and home and to provide the students with an opportunity to watch their debate afterward for reflection.
- ◆ Students tweet the debate live using the hashtag unique to the debate; e.g., the homework debate utilized the hashtag #hwdebate.
- ◆ Students persevere at a distinguished level; all students actively engaged learning at their highest, differentiated level.
- ◆ Rubrics are sent by judges, allowing for reflection by teachers, administrators, and students for future argument/debate learning. All students and teachers are winners, no matter the rubric score.

Takeaways from Melissa's Story

This unit of study addresses a plethora of Common Core State Standards, with a direct emphasis on the first writing anchor standard, argument writing. This particular learning experience is advantageous for students on three fronts. The students learn the parliamentary debate structure and methods, as well as the technology used to enhance and engage with the other schools, and the students research the topic at hand. The students and teachers are acquiring the essential skills needed in the twenty-first-century digital age, by becoming digital citizens, by engaging in digital communication, by telling their digital story, by fostering connected teaching culture, and by bringing a new purpose and thinking to the teaching and learning in the classroom.

In the end this learning progression won the 2013 Edublogs Award for "Best Use of Videos and Media" in the classroom. It is also showcased as one of the best practices for the usage of technology in the classroom in the upcoming PBS documentary, investigated by PBS *NewsHour* education correspondent John Merrow, "School Sleuth: The Case of the Wired Classroom," which premiered at the Digital Learning Day convention in Washington, DC, on March 13, 2015.

Find out more information about this learning opportunity and how it continues to transform across classrooms and across states each year.[6]

What Will Your Story Be?

Being an educator today requires us to prepare our students for a rapidly changing world. How does one adequately prepare students for jobs that don't even exist yet? What skills will our students need for their futures? As John Dewey said, "If we teach today's students as we taught yesterday, we rob them of tomorrow."

The Framework for 21st Century Learning includes the 4Cs—critical thinking, communication, collaboration, and creativity. The authors have strived to share with you ways to get your students collaborating with others, which in turn will lead to improved communication, critical thinking, and creativity skills.

Billy, Jerry, and Paula encourage you, if you haven't already done so, to start building a PLN. Establishing a PLN is just the first step to becoming a connected educator and leads to opportunities to connect your students to the world. Today's children are constantly plugged into some type of tech device. It is the job of teachers to show them how to use their devices for educational purposes. Having your students collaborate is very important in the world in which we live in today.

Find a simple collaborative project to begin with and try not to over-think it. Just getting started is sometimes the hardest step along the journey. Start by sending a tweet, joining a Google+ community, or using some other social media community to find a connection. No matter your comfort level with technology, there are all types of projects out there, so break out of your comfort zone and connect!

Notes

1. www.ncs-tech.org/?p=4620.
2. www.stager.tv/blog/.
3. www.voicethread.com/myvoice/#thread/809450/4319530.
4. www.bsherry.wordpress.com/2009/12/17/collaboration-brewing-in-my-twitter-network/.
5. www.livebinders.com/play/play?id=818758.
6. www.virtualdebate.weebly.com/.

Glossary

#4thchat—A Twitter chat composed mainly of fourth-grade teachers who share ideas, lessons, and projects. The actual chat is Mondays at 8:00 p.m. (EST).

100th Day of School—The 100th day of school is the opportunity to create activities based on the number 100. Schools celebrate this event at different times (see Chapter 5).

Acceptable Use Policy—Acceptable or Fair Use Policy is a set of rules on the use of technology in schools.

Animoto—Animoto is a site that creates videos from photographs.

backchannel—Backchannel is a digital conversation that happens at the same time as a face-to-face activity.

blog—A blog or weblog is an online journal or diary in which you can express your thoughts and ideas to a global audience.

body language—Body language includes the nonverbal forms of how we communicate, such as our posture, facial expressions, touch, the way we walk, stand, sit, etc.

BYOD (Bring Your Own Device)—BYOD is a trend that many schools now allow. Students can bring their own tech devices to school.

close reading—Close reading asks students to really analyze text they are reading to notice the language and features that the author employs.

collaboration—Working together to accomplish a task is collaboration.

Common Core State Standards—These are a set of high-quality academic expectations in English language arts (ELA) and mathematics that define the knowledge and skills all students should master by the end of each grade level in order to be on track for success in college and career.

Commonwealth Day—Commonwealth Day is a celebration of the Commonwealth of Nations that is held on the second Monday in March.

connected educators and connected students—Being connected means using the Internet and tech tools to reach out to others to share and learn with one another.

critical thinking—Critical thinking is the ability to analyze information and come up with a reasonable conclusion.

cultural responsiveness—Cultural responsiveness is being able to include cultural references in all aspects of learning and respect the cultures of all peoples.

database—A database is a computer-generated way to store data.

deductive reasoning—A process of reasoning to reach a logical conclusion.

digital citizenship—Parents and educators need to teach children about the responsible use of technology devices and how to be a good citizen in our digital world.

digital footprint—A digital footprint is the trail of the information that you put online and that stays online.

digital literacy—To be digitally literate one has to be able to find, understand, evaluate, create, and communicate digital information.

Dot Day—International Dot Day on September 15 is a worldwide celebration of creativity. It was inspired by the children's book *The Dot* by Peter H. Reynolds.

e-book—An e-book is an electronic version of a printed book. It can consist of not only words but pictures as well. E-books can contain clickable or hypertext links to get to sites.

edcamps—Edcamps are unconferences where participants choose the topics they want to present on and can select the sessions they want to attend or lead.

Edmodo—Edmodo is a closed social learning network that allows students to connect, learn, and share safely.

Email Around the World—A 1999–2000 project coordinated by Tammy Payton that connected classes all around the world by email.

exit slips—At the conclusion of a lesson or project, students submit on a piece of paper what they have learned.

flat classroom—Using web tools that enable communication, collaboration, and interaction has allowed classrooms to open their doors to the world easily.

Flat Stanley—The Flat Stanley Project started in 1995 and was inspired by the book *Flat Stanley*, written by Jeff Brown. The project includes keeping track of the travels of Flat Stanley by letter-writing. Students today take pictures of Flat Stanley in different locations where they live or travel to.

Four Cs (4Cs)—The twenty-first-century skills that many people feel were most important for K-12 learners were determined to be collaboration, communication, creativity, and critical thinking. Others have also included connectivity.

Global Read Aloud—The Global Read Aloud Project began in 2010 having children read one book aloud and then make connections around the world.

Glogster—A multimedia platform that allows students to use a variety of media to demonstrate their learning.

Google Classroom—Google Classroom enables teachers to use the myriad of Google tools such as Google Docs, Google Drive, and Gmail to have their students work on assignments, provide feedback, and communicate with them.

Google Documents/Google Docs—These web-based documents allow for people all over the world to simultaneously work on Word documents, spreadsheets, and forms of presentation collaboratively.

Google Hangouts—A free videoconferencing tool that allows up to ten participants to connect, learn, and share with one another.

Google+—A social network website through Google.

hashtag (#)—A hashtag is used to mark keywords or topics in a tweet or other forms of social media.

Hispanic Heritage Month—Each year from September 15 through October 15, Hispanic culture is celebrated.

hotspot—A hotspot is a location that offers Internet access over a wireless local area network.

interactive whiteboard—An interactive whiteboard (IWB) is a display connected to a computer to project the page on a screen, and students can interact with the display using the board's pen or dry erase markers.

ISTE—International Society of Technology in Education is the premier nonprofit organization serving educators and education leaders committed to empowering connected learners in a connected world.

ISTE Standards—Formerly known as the NETS, the ISTE Standards are standards for learning, teaching, and leading in the digital age.

Labor Day—In the United States on the first Monday in September, this day celebrates the American Labor Movement. Labor Day in many other countries is celebrated at different times.

makerspace—Makerspaces are areas set aside in libraries and schools to allow children to learn and create.

microexpressions—Observing a person's face and their expressions such as a smile or scowl can be helpful in judging their mood.

Mystery Location Call—Two or more classes in different states or countries try to find out where the other is located. The call can usually be done by Skype or Google Hangout.

netiquette—Using netiquette, the online form of etiquette, means being a responsible and proper user of the Internet.

NETS—NETS is the former name used for the ISTE Standards for learning, teaching, and leading in the digital age.

Next Generation Science Standards (NGSS)—The National Research Council (NRC), the National Science Teachers Association (NSTA), the American Association for the Advancement of Science (AAAS), and Achieve developed the Next Generation Science Standards.

O.R.E.O. (Our Really Exciting Online) Project—This project involves stacking Oreo cookies and calculating statistics for the results.

Padlet—Padlet is an online bulletin board.

Personal (or Professional) Learning Network(PLN)—A personal learning network is your collection of people that you learn and share with. A professional learning network is a group of people in your field.

photosynthesis—The conversion of light energy (sunlight) into chemical energy and storing it in the bonds of sugar.

Pi Day—On March 14 (3/14) we celebrate the ratio of the circumference of a circle to its diameter, which is approximately 3.14159.

Plimoth Plantation—Plimoth Plantation in Plymouth, Massachusetts, is a re-creation of the original settlement of the Plymouth Colony. The historical interpreters stay in the character of people living in the seventeenth century.

PowerPoint—A PowerPoint is a slide show presentation. The PowerPoint program was created by Microsoft.

QR Code—Abbreviated from Quick Response Code, a QR code is the trademark for a type of matrix barcode (or two-dimensional barcode) first designed for the automotive industry in Japan. A barcode is a machine-readable optical label that contains information about the item to which it is attached.

Read Across America—March 2, Dr. Seuss's birthday, is a nationwide reading celebration that occurs every year.

Remembrance Day—Similar to Memorial Day in the United States, Remembrance Day is celebrated in Commonwealth of Nations member states to remember those who gave up their lives while serving in the armed forces.

Remind—Remind is a free, safe messaging service for teachers to communicate with students and parents via text or email.

September 11, 2001—On September 11, 2001, the Islamic terrorist group al-Qaeda carried out four attacks on the United States using hijacked airplanes. The World Trade Center Towers in New York City were destroyed by two airplanes, the Pentagon in Washington, D.C., was hit by another, and a fourth plane was downed in Pennsylvania.

Skype—A tool to use for video and voice calls as well as instant messaging and file sharing.

social media—Internet tools like Twitter, Facebook, Pinterest, Instagram, and Google+ that let people share information, pictures, and ideas.

spreadsheet—A spreadsheet is an interactive, computer-generated way to organize, analyze, and store data.

Travel Buddies—Travel buddies are objects like a paper Flat Stanley, stuffed animals, or other items that are sent to other schools.

Twitter—Twitter is a social networking platform that connects people all over the world. The basic tweet is only 140 characters.

Twitter educational chats—There are educational chats on Twitter seven days a week for most grade levels, subject areas, interests, and states. There are chats for students, teachers, administrators, and parents.

URL—A URL is a Uniform Resource Locator or a web address.

Ustream—Ustream is a company that provides video streaming services.

videoconferencing—Videoconferencing enables two or more locations to communicate visually and with voice simultaneously with one another.

virtual debates—Classes in different locations carry out a debate on a topic via Skype or Google Hangouts.

Virtual Field Trips (VFT)—Virtual Field Trips are guided educational on-line journeys.

VoiceThread—This is an interactive tool that allows the sharing of comments, images, and documents.

Voxer—Voxer is a messaging app for a smartphone that is similar to a walkie-talkie but also allows for text and pictures.

webcam—A webcam is a video camera attached to a computer that allows the transmission of picture and audio.

WebQuest—Web quests are lessons where the information has been gathered from the internet.

webinars—Webinars are web-based seminars transmitted using videoconferencing software.

wiki—A wiki, similar to a blog, is a website that is a collaboration of works contributed by multiple authors.

Yammer—Yammer is a private social network that helps people connect.

YouTube—YouTube is a video-sharing site that provides a lot of how-to information.

Appendix A

Standards Correlation Charts

Correlation Chart for the Common Core State Standards

The projects that we have participated in are denoted by an asterisk (*).

Collaborative Project or Idea	Anchor Standards for Common Core State Standards, K-8
Chapter 2	
Mystery Location Call*, p. 9	RI.6
	RL.1
	RF
	SL
Chapter 3	
Sharing a Guest Speaker: Veterinarian Live*, p. 24	SL
Sharing a Guest Speaker: Celebrating the Constitution*, p. 26	SL

The Olympics, p. 27	SL
Olympic Game Show Quiz, p.28	RI
	W
	SL
Math Competition, p. 29	SL
	OA
	MD
	NBT
	MD
	G
Science Fair Challenge, p. 29	W.6
	W.7
	W.8
	W.9
	MD
	G
Dry Ice Experiment*, p. 30	SL
Chapter 4	
Labor Day, p. 39	RI.9
	W.2
	W.7
	SL
O.R.E.O. (Our Really Exciting Online) Project*, p. 39	MD.1
	MD.2
	MD.9
	CC
	SL

September 11: Showing Compassion, p. 41	RI.6
	RL.1
	W.1
	W.2
	W.3
	SL
Hispanic Heritage Month (September 15–October 15), p. 41	RI.6
	RL.1
	W.2
	SL
International Dot Day*, p. 42	RL.1
	RL.2
	RL.3
	RL.6
	RL.7
	W.6
	SL
	CC
	MD
Global Read Aloud*, p. 43	RL
	W
	SL
How Weather Affects Us*, p. 44	W
	SL
	MD.4
	MD.10
	NBT.1

	OA.1
	OA.2
Pumpkin Seed Project*, p. 45	RI
	W
	SL
	NBT
	OA.1
	MD.4
	MD.10
Halloween Projects, p. 45	RI
	RL
	W.3
Election Day, p. 46	RI
	W.3
	SL
	NBT.4
	OA.1
	CC
Veterans Day/Remembrance Day, p. 46	RI.6
	W.2
	SL
Gettysburg Address*, p. 47	RI
	SL
Native American Heritage Month, p. 47	RI.6
	RL.1
	W.2
	SL

Thanksgiving Day: Canada (October) vs. the United States (November), p. 47	RI.6
	W.2
	SL
Plimoth Plantation*, p. 48	RI
	W
	SL
Chapter 5	
100th Day of School*, p. 51	RI.5
	W.4
	W.5
	W.6
	SL
	CC
	NBT
	OA
	MD
	G
Holiday Card Exchange*, p. 52	W.4
	W.5
	W.6
	SL
RACK—Random Acts of Christmas Kindness*, p. 53	RI.6
	W.5
	W.6
	W.7
	SL

Pearl Harbor Day, p. 54	RI. 6
	RL.1
	RL.3
	RL.6
	W.2
	W.4
	W.5
	W.6
	W.9
	SL
	MD
12.12.12 Blogging Challenge*, p. 54	W.3
	W.5
	W.6
	SL
New Year's, p. 55	W.3
	SL
Dr. Martin Luther King Jr.*, p. 55	RI.6
	W.2
	W.7
	SL
Martin's Big Words*, p. 56	RI.1
	SL
American Heart Month*, p. 57	RI.6
	W.2
	CC
	NBT
	MD

Black History Month*, p. 58	RI.6
	W.2
	W.3
	W.4
	W.5
	W.6
	W.7
	SL
Groundhog Day, p. 58	RI. 6
	W.6
	W.7
	SL
	MD.4
	MD.9
Super Bowl Connections*, p. 58	RI.6
	W.6
	W.7
	SL
	MD.4
	MD.9
Presidents' Day, p. 60	RI.6
	W.2
	W.4
	W.5
	W.6
	W.7
	SL

Snow Days, p. 61	W.3
	W.6
	OA
	MD
Mardi Gras*, p. 61	RI.6
	W.2
	W.4
	W.5
	W.6
	SL
Read Across America—Dr. Seuss's Birthday*, p. 62	RL
	SL
Commonwealth Day, p. 63	W
	SL
Pi Day—March 14 (3/14), p. 63	RI.6
	RL.1
	RL.5
	W.2
	W.7
	SL
	MD
	G
St. Patrick's Day*, p. 63	RI
	RL
	W
	SL
	CC

	OA
	MD
Women's History Month, p. 64	RI.6
	RL.1
	W.2
	W.7
	SL
Chapter 6	
National Autism Awareness Month, p. 66	RI.6
	W.6
	W.7
	SL
Standardized Testing*, p. 67	RI.6
	W
	SL
PictureIt Project*, p. 68	RI
	SL
	CC
	MD
	G
Impromptu Calls*, p. 68	RI
	RL
	W
	SL
Poetry Month*, p. 69	RI
	RL
	W
	SL

April Fools' Day, p. 70	W.4
	W.6
	SL
Baseball, p. 70	RI
	RL
	W
	SL
	NBT
	MD
	G
Holocaust Remembrance Day, p. 71	RI.1
	RI.3
	RI.6
	RL.1
	RL.6
	RL.7
	W.2
	W.5
	W.6
	W.7
	SL
Earth Day—Grocery Bag Project*, p. 72	RI
	W
	SL
	MD.4
	MD.9

Arbor Day, p. 73	RI.6
	W.7
	W.9
	MD.4
	MD.9
National Inventors Month, p. 73	RI.6
	W.7
	SL
	MD.4
	MD.9
10-Day Passion Challenge and Identity Day*, p. 73	W
	SL
Cinco de Mayo*, p. 74	RI.6
	W
	SL
Memorial Day, p. 75	RI
	W
	SL
Flag Day, p. 75	RI
	W
	SL
Graduation—End of School, p. 75	W
	SL

Correlation Chart for the ISTE Standards for Students

The projects that we have participated in are denoted by an asterisk (*).

Collaborative Project or Idea	ISTE Standards for Students
Chapter 2	
Mystery Location Call, p. 9	2, 3, 5, 6
Chapter 3	
Sharing a Guest Speaker: Veterinarian Live*, p. 24	2, 5
Sharing a Guest Speaker: Celebrating the Constitution*, p. 26	2, 5
The Olympics, p. 27	2, 3, 5
Olympic Game Show Quiz, p.28	2, 3, 4
Math Competition, p. 29	2, 3, 4
Science Fair Challenge, p. 29	2, 3, 5, 6
Dry Ice Experiment*, p. 30	2, 3, 5, 6
Chapter 4	
Labor Day, p. 39	2, 3, 5, 6
O.R.E.O. (Our Really Exciting Online) Project*, p. 39	2, 3, 5, 6
September 11: Showing Compassion, p. 41	2, 3, 5, 6
Hispanic Heritage Month (September 15–October 15), p. 41	2, 3, 5, 6
International Dot Day*, p. 42	2, 3, 5, 6
Global Read Aloud*, p. 43	1, 2, 3, 5, 6
How Weather Affects Us*, p. 44	1, 2, 3, 4, 5, 6
Pumpkin Seed Project*, p. 45	1, 2, 3, 5, 6
Halloween Projects, p. 45	1, 2, 3, 4, 5, 6
Election Day, p. 46	1, 2, 3, 5, 6
Veterans Day/Remembrance Day, p. 46	2, 3, 5

Gettysburg Address*, p. 47	2, 3, 5
Native American Heritage Month, p. 47	2, 3, 5, 6
Thanksgiving Day: Canada (October) vs. the United States (November), p. 47	2, 3, 5, 6
Plimoth Plantation*, p. 48	2, 3, 5
Chapter 5	
100th Day of School, p. 51	2, 3, 5, 6
Holiday Card Exchange*, p. 52	2, 3, 5, 6
RACK—Random Acts of Christmas Kindness*, p. 53	1, 2, 3, 4, 5, 6
Pearl Harbor Day, p. 54	1, 2, 3, 4, 5, 6
12.12.12 Blogging Challenge*, p. 54	1, 2, 3, 4, 5, 6
New Year's, p. 55	2, 3, 4, 5
Dr. Martin Luther King Jr., p. 55	2, 3, 4, 5, 6
Martin's Big Words*, p. 56	2, 5, 6
American Heart Month*, p. 57	2, 5
Black History Month*, p. 58	1, 2, 3, 4, 5, 6
Groundhog Day, p. 58	1, 2, 3, 4, 5, 6
Super Bowl Connections*, p. 58	2, 3, 4, 5, 6
Presidents' Day, p. 60	1, 2, 3, 4, 5, 6
Snow Days, p. 61	2, 4, 5, 6
Mardi Gras*, p. 61	2, 3, 5, 6
Read Across America—Dr. Seuss's Birthday*, p. 62	2, 5, 6
Commonwealth Day, p. 63	2, 3, 4
Pi Day—March 14 (3/14), p. 63	2, 3, 5, 6
St. Patrick's Day*, p. 63	2, 3, 5, 6
Women's History Month, p. 64	2, 3, 6
Chapter 6	
National Autism Awareness Month, p. 66	2, 3, 5, 6

Standardized Testing*, p. 67	1, 2, 5, 6
PictureIt Project*, p. 68	2, 5, 6
Impromptu Calls*, p. 68	1, 2, 5, 6
Poetry Month*, p. 69	2, 5, 6
April Fools' Day, p. 70	2, 5, 6
Baseball, p. 70	1, 2, 3, 4, 5, 6
Holocaust Remembrance Day, p. 71	2, 3, 5, 6
Earth Day—Grocery Bag Project*, p. 72	1, 2, 3, 4, 5, 6
Arbor Day, p. 73	2, 4, 5, 6
National Inventors Month, p. 73	1, 2, 3, 4, 5, 6
10-Day Passion Challenge and Identity Day*, p. 73	2, 3, 4, 5
Cinco de Mayo*, p. 74	2, 3, 4, 5
Memorial Day, p. 75	2, 3, 5, 6
Flag Day, p. 75	2, 3, 5, 6
Graduation—End of School, p. 75	2, 5, 6

Correlation Chart for the ISTE Standards for Teachers

The projects that we have participated in are denoted by an asterisk (*).

Collaborative Project or Idea	ISTE Standards for Teacher
Mystery Location Call, p. 9	1, 2, 3, 4
Chapter 3	
Sharing a Guest Speaker: Veterinarian Live*, p. 24	1, 2, 3, 4
Sharing a Guest Speaker: Celebrating the Constitution*, p. 26	1, 2, 3, 4
The Olympics, p. 27	1, 2, 3, 4
Olympic Game Show Quiz*, p. 28	1, 2, 3, 4

Math Competition, p. 29	1, 2, 3, 4
Science Fair Challenge, p. 29	1, 2, 3
Dry Ice Experiment*, p. 30	1, 2, 3
Chapter 4	
Labor Day, p. 39	1, 2
O.R.E.O. (Our Really Exciting Online) Project*, p. 39	1, 2, 3, 4
September 11: Showing Compassion, p. 41	1, 2, 3, 4
Hispanic Heritage Month (September 15–October 15), p. 41	1, 2, 3, 4
International Dot Day*, p. 42	1, 2, 3, 4
Global Read Aloud*, p. 43	1, 2, 3, 4
How Weather Affects Us*, p. 44	1, 2, 3, 4
Pumpkin Seed Project*, p. 45	1, 2, 3, 4
Halloween Projects, p. 45	1, 2, 3, 4
Election Day, p. 46	1, 2, 3, 4
Veterans Day/Remembrance Day, p. 46	1, 2, 3, 4
Gettysburg Address, p. 47	1, 2, 3, 4
Native American Heritage Month, p. 47	1, 2, 3, 4
Thanksgiving Day: Canada (October) vs. the United States (November), p. 47	1, 2, 3, 4
Plimoth Plantation*, p. 48	1, 2, 3, 4, 5
Chapter 5	
100th Day of School, p. 51	1, 2, 3, 4
Holiday Card Exchange*, p. 52	1, 2, 3, 4
RACK—Random Acts of Christmas Kindness*, p. 53	1, 2, 3, 4
Pearl Harbor Day, p. 54	1, 2, 3, 4
12.12.12 Blogging Challenge*, p. 54	1, 2, 3, 4
New Year's, p. 55	1, 2, 3, 4
Dr. Martin Luther King Jr., p. 55	1, 2, 3, 4
Martin's Big Words*, p. 56	2, 3, 4

American Heart Month*, p. 57	2, 3, 4
Black History Month*, p. 58	2, 3, 4
Groundhog Day, p. 58	1, 2, 3, 4
Super Bowl Connections*, p. 58	1, 2, 3, 4
Presidents' Day, p. 60	1, 2, 3, 4
Snow Days, p. 61	1, 2, 3, 4
Mardi Gras*, p. 61	1, 2, 3, 4
Read Across America—Dr. Seuss's Birthday*, p. 62	1, 2, 3, 4
Commonwealth Day, p. 63	1, 2, 3, 4
Pi Day—March 14 (3/14), p. 63	1, 2, 3, 4
St. Patrick's Day*, p. 63	1, 2, 3, 4
Women's History Month, p. 64	1, 2, 3, 4
Chapter 6	
National Autism Awareness Month, p. 66	1, 2, 3, 4
Standardized Testing*, p. 67	1, 2, 3, 4
PictureIt Project*, p. 68	1, 2, 3, 4
Impromptu Calls*, p. 68	1, 2, 3, 4, 5
Poetry Month*, p. 69	1, 2, 3, 4
April Fools' Day, p. 70	1, 2, 3, 4
Baseball, p. 70	1, 2, 3, 4
Holocaust Remembrance Day, p. 71	1, 2, 3, 4
Earth Day—Grocery Bag Project*, p. 72	1, 2, 3, 4
Arbor Day, p. 73	1, 2, 3, 4
National Inventors Month, p. 73	1, 2, 3, 4
10-Day Passion Challenge and Identity Day*, p. 73	1, 2, 3, 4
Cinco de Mayo*, p. 74	1, 2, 3, 4
Memorial Day, p. 75	1, 2, 3, 4
Flag Day, p. 75	1, 2, 3, 4

| Graduation—End of School, p. 75 | 1, 2, 3, 4 |
| Summer Projects, p. 76 | 1, 2, 3, 4, 5 |

Correlation Chart for the Next Generation Science Standards

The projects that we have participated in are denoted by an asterisk (*).

Collaborative Project or Idea	Next Generation Science Standards
Chapter 3	
Science Fair Challenge, p. 29	PS
	LS
	ESS
Dry Ice Experiment*, p. 30	PS1A
	PS1B
Chapter 4	
How Weather Affects Us*, p. 44	ESS2D
	ESS3C
	ESS3D
	LS1
	LS2
Pumpkin Seed Project*, p. 45	LS1
	LS2
Chapter 5	
Groundhog Day, p. 58	ESS2
	ESS3
Snow Days, p. 61	ESS2
	ESS3

Chapter 6	
Earth Day—Grocery Bag Project, p. 72	ESS2
	ESS3
Arbor Day, p. 73	ESS2
	ESS3
National Inventors Month, p. 73	PS2
	PS3
	PS4
	ETS

Appendix B
Key Standards

The ISTE National Education Technology Standards (NETS*S) and Performance Indicators for Students

1. **Creativity and Innovation**

   Students demonstrate creative thinking, construct knowledge, and develop innovative products and processes using technology. Students:

   a. apply existing knowledge to generate new ideas, products, or processes;
   b. create original work as a means of personal or group expression;
   c. use models and simulations to explore complex systems and issues;
   d. identify trends and forecast possibilities.

2. **Communication and Collaboration**

   Students use digital media and environments to communicate and work collaboratively, including at a distance, to support individual learning and contribute to learning of others. Students:

   a. interact, collaborate, and publish with peers, experts, or others employing a variety of digital environments and media;

   b. communicate information and ideas effectively to multiple
      audiences using a variety of media and formats;
   c. develop cultural understanding and global awareness by
      engaging with learners of other cultures;
   d. contribute to project teams to produce original works or solve
      problems.

3. **Research and Information Fluency**
   Students apply digital tools to gather, evaluate, and use information. Students:

   a. plan strategies to guide inquiry;
   b. locate, organize, analyze, evaluate, synthesize, and ethically
      use information from a variety of sources and media;
   c. evaluate and select information sources and digital tools based
      on the appropriateness to specific tasks;
   d. process data and report results.

4. **Critical Thinking, Problem Solving, and Decision Making**
   Students use critical thinking skills to plan and conduct research,
   manage projects, solve problems, and make informed decisions
   using appropriate digital tools and resources. Students:

   a. identify and define authentic problems and significant
      questions for investigation;
   b. plan and manage activities to develop a solution or complete a
      project;
   c. collect and analyze data to identify solutions and/or make
      informed decisions;
   d. use multiple processes and diverse perspectives to explore
      alternative solutions.

5. **Digital Citizenship**
   Students understand human, cultural, and societal issues related to
   technology and practice legal and ethical behavior. Students:

   a. advocate and practice safe, legal, and responsible use of
      information and technology;
   b. exhibit a positive attitude toward using technology that
      supports collaboration, learning, and productivity;

    c. demonstrate personal responsibility for lifelong learning;
    d. exhibit leadership for digital citizenship.

6. **Technology Operations and Concepts**
Students demonstrate a sound understanding of technology concepts, systems, and operations. Students:

    a. understand and use technology systems;
    b. select and use applications effectively and productively;
    c. troubleshoot systems and applications;
    d. transfer current knowledge to learning of new technologies.

The ISTE National Education Technology Standards (NETS*T) and Performance Indicators for Teachers

Effective teachers model and apply the ISTE Standards for Students as they design, implement, and assess learning experiences to engage students and improve learning; enrich professional practice; and provide positive models for students, colleagues, and the community. All teachers should meet the following standards and performance indicators.

1. **Facilitate and Inspire Student Learning and Creativity**
Teachers use their knowledge of subject matter, teaching and learning, and technology to facilitate experiences that advance student learning, creativity, and innovation in both face-to-face and virtual environments. Teachers will:

    a. promote, support, and model creative and innovative thinking and inventiveness;
    b. engage students in exploring real-world issues and solving authentic problems using digital tools and resources;
    c. promote student reflection using collaborative tools to reveal and clarify students' conceptual understanding and thinking, planning, and creative processes;
    d. model collaborative knowledge construction by engaging in learning with students, colleagues, and others in face-to-face and virtual environments.

2. **Design and Develop Digital-Age Learning Experiences and Assessments**

    Teachers design, develop, and evaluate authentic learning experiences and assessments incorporating contemporary tools and resources to maximize content learning in context and to develop the knowledge, skills, and attitudes identified in the Standards. Teachers will:

    a. design or adapt relevant learning experiences that incorporate digital tools and resources to promote student learning and creativity;
    b. develop technology-enriched learning environments that enable all students to pursue their individual curiosities and become active participants in setting their own educational goals, managing their own learning, and assessing their own progress;
    c. customize and personalize learning activities to address students' diverse learning styles, working strategies, and abilities using digital tools and resources;
    d. provide students with multiple and varied formative and summative assessments aligned with content and technology standards, and use resulting data to inform learning and teaching.

3. **Model Digital-Age Work and Learning**

    Teachers exhibit knowledge, skills, and work processes representative of an innovative professional in a global and digital society. Teachers will:

    a. demonstrate fluency in technology systems and the transfer of current knowledge to new technologies and situations;
    b. collaborate with students, peers, parents, and community members using digital tools and resources to support student success and innovation;
    c. communicate relevant information and ideas effectively to students, parents, and peers using a variety of digital-age media and formats;
    d. model and facilitate effective use of current and emerging digital tools to locate, analyze, evaluate, and use information resources to support research and learning.

4. **Promote and Model Digital Citizenship and Responsibility**
   Teachers understand local and global societal issues and responsibilities in an evolving digital culture and exhibit legal and ethical behavior in their professional practices. Teachers will:

   a. advocate, model, and teach safe, legal, and ethical use of digital information and technology, including respect for copyright, intellectual property, and the appropriate documentation of sources;
   b. address the diverse needs of all learners by using learner-centered strategies providing equitable access to appropriate digital tools and resources;
   c. promote and model digital etiquette and responsible social interactions related to the use of technology and information;
   d. develop and model cultural understanding and global awareness by engaging with colleagues and students of other cultures using digital-age communication and collaboration tools.

5. **Engage in Professional Growth and Leadership**
   Teachers continuously improve their professional practice, model lifelong learning, and exhibit leadership in their school and professional community by promoting and demonstrating the effective use of digital tools and resources. Teachers will:

   a. participate in local and global learning communities to explore creative applications of technology to improve student learning;
   b. exhibit leadership by demonstrating a vision of technology infusion, participating in shared decision making and community building, and developing the leadership and technology skills of others;
   c. evaluate and reflect on current research and professional practice on a regular basis to make effective use of existing and emerging digital tools and resources in support of student learning;
   d. contribute to the effectiveness, vitality, and self-renewal of the teaching profession and of their school and community.

Appendix C

Flat Stanley Lesson Plan

Day 1
Reading: Chapters 1 & 2
Vocabulary or Word Work Arthur, tailor, Jeffreys, fragile
Before Reading Set a purpose for reading—Today we will read to meet Stanley, a very interesting character. He starts out as an ordinary boy. Let's find out what happens to Stanley and if he stays as ordinary as he starts! Good readers try to remember details about the text as they continue to read more and more of the story.
After Reading *Text-Dependent Questions* What can Flat Stanley do because he is flat? Why does Stanley's mother take him to the doctor? What is Stanley's response when Dr. Dan asks him how he feels? What does Dr. Dan recommend? What does the nurse do before Stanley leaves Dr. Dan's office?

Non-Text-Dependent Questions
Stanley's brother Arthur is a little jealous of Stanley's flatness. Would you be?

Writing Response
Some people find it safer to carry on as usual after something extraordinary has happened. In the story, Stanley's mother takes him to the doctor to have him checked out. Write a paragraph describing what happens at the doctor's office.

---

*Send home parent note asking for an address to mail their child's Stanley. Find an address to mail the class Stanley (one that is trusted since this one will be tracked).

Day 2

Reading: Chapter 3

Vocabulary or Word Work
apologize, Encyclopedia Britannica, phases

Before Reading
Set a purpose for reading—In the story today, Arthur is starting to get a little jealous of Stanley. Stanley decides to do something nice for Arthur, but he ends up regretting it. Read to find out what happens to Stanley when Arthur thinks only of himself.

After Reading
Text-Dependent Questions
How does Stanley get in and out of rooms now that he is flat?
Where does Stanley go to visit his friend? How does he get there and back?
How does Stanley stay safe in crowds on Sunday outings?
How does Stanley use his flatness to help others?
What can you infer about Arthur when he says "Phooey!"?
Non-Text-Dependent Questions
How do you feel about Arthur taking off and leaving Stanley in the air? Who was Arthur thinking of at that time? Have you ever had a similar situation?

Writing Response

Often, there are advantages to finding yourself in a new and different condition. Being flat allows Stanley to do some pretty unusual things. Write a paragraph relating some of the things Stanley is able to do because he is flat.

---

*Begin making Flat Stanley for your class. Make one larger/sturdier Stanley to be mailed and tracked for the class as a whole, and allow students to make an individual Stanley.

Day 3
Reading: Chapter 4
Vocabulary or Word Work thieves, permission, disguise, shepherdesses
Before Reading Character—Readers think about how characters change throughout the story. How has Stanley changed or other characters changed so far? Keep looking for ways that characters change.
After Reading *Text-Dependent Questions* List two reasons the museum is hard to guard. What was Stanley's idea to catch the crooks? How did Stanley feel about the disguise? How do you know? What did the thieves think they needed when Stanley yelled for the police? How was Stanley rewarded? *Non-Text-Dependent Questions* Were you able to make any connections to the story? (text to self, text to text, text to world)
Writing Response Sometimes characters have to make the best of a bad situation. Stanley is flat, but it allows him to do some incredible things. Write about how Stanley got an idea to guard the museum and how he was able to help save the day.

---

*Write a class letter to go with the class Stanley on his adventure. Make a form letter for students to fill in with their information for their personal Stanley.

© 2016, *Connecting Your Students with the World*, B. Krakower, P. Naugle and J. Blumengarten, Routledge

Day 4
Reading: Chapter 5
Vocabulary or Word Work religion, rummage, bulged
Before Reading Character—In this chapter Arthur feels really bad for his brother. He comes up with an idea on how to help Stanley. Read the chapter to find out what Arthur does to help Stanley. Readers think about how characters change throughout the story. How has Stanley changed or other characters changed so far? Keep looking for ways that characters change.
After Reading *Text-Dependent Questions* By the end of the story, how does Stanley feel about being flat? Why have his feelings changed? How does Arthur comfort Stanley? What is Arthur's good idea to help Stanley? By the end of the story, how does Arthur's idea work out? *Non-Text-Dependent Questions* Did the story end as you expected?
Writing Response A person facing an unpleasant situation can become discouraged and benefit from help. At the end of the story, Arthur has a good idea for helping Stanley. Write a paragraph describing Arthur's good idea. Your paragraph should tell how Arthur comes up with this idea.

---

*Mail Stanley and help students mail their Stanley as well. Show the website where visitors can upload their Stanley information to share with the class. Keep track of visits on a class map. (Note: A new website is created each year for this project; a web search should direct you to the most current.)

Additional Writing Prompts/Discussion Questions

Imagine that Stanley is your friend in real life. Write words and phrases that would help you describe him to someone who didn't know him. (What does Stanley look like? What kind of personality does he have? What does he like to do?)

Compare and contrast Stanley with Arthur or another character in the book.

How does Arthur feel about his brother Stanley's situation? Write a paragraph about Arthur's reactions to Stanley's flatness. Be sure to include details that show how Arthur feels.

In the story, the policemen call Mrs. Lambchop a "cuckoo." The policemen apologize when they realize they have made a mistake. Mrs. Lambchop says that people should think twice before making rude remarks. The policemen think this is a good rule.

Think about a good rule you think everyone should follow. Write a paragraph about a rule you think everyone should follow. (Ch. 2)

In the story, Stanley Lambchop has some good ideas about how to use his changed shape to help others. Think about a time that you had an idea to help others. Write a paragraph describing a time you came up with an idea that you used to help others. (Ch. 3)

Some Stanley Links

www.teachingideas.co.uk/library/books/flatstanley.htm
www.flatstanleybooks.com/
www.flatstanley.com/
Lessons Adapted from www.bookpunch.com (Lesson Plan Aid for Flat Stanley)
Guided Reading Lesson Plan M: www.flatstanley.koolkidssign.com/FS2.pdf

Flat Stanley Project

Dear Families,

We are reading *Flat Stanley* in first grade. Stanley is a little boy who becomes flat. He is able to be mailed to visit a friend in another state.

We are making a Flat Stanley at school for each child to mail. Please help us by providing an address of a family member or friend for your child to mail their Stanley to.

Name: _____

Street: _____

City: _____   State: _____   Zip: _____

We will also take donations of stamps to mail our letters. If you can send a stamp or two to help get all the Stanleys in the mail, that would be appreciated!

Please return address and stamps by *Thursday*!

—The First-Grade Teachers

Dear _____,

This is my Flat Stanley. I made him after reading the book *Flat Stanley* with

my first-grade class. My favorite part of the book was _____

_____. What I like

best about Stanley is _____.

We are sending Stanley on an adventure around the globe. Please take some photos with Stanley and write about his adventures with you. Then return Stanley and the information to me at:

Daphne Elementary School
2307 Main Street
Daphne, AL 36526

c/o _____ in _____ 's class

Thank you for helping me with the project. I hope you and Stanley have fun together!

Sincerely,

_____

Original Mailing: September 8, 2014

Dear Friends,

Our class has read *Flat Stanley*. Poor Stanley was flattened when a bulletin board fell on him. The good news is now he can travel the world in an envelope. Please spend some time with Stanley and take some pictures of your adventures together. **Then visit http://goo.gl/WVeOWA and upload what you have done.** We will add you to our virtual interactive map and see where Stanley has gone on his travels.

When you are done, **please send Stanley on to another location** so the adventure can continue! Include this letter so they will have directions on what to do with Stanley. You can see where Stanley has been on our map at https://goo.gl/maps/mL5jg.

If you want to share other items with us, you can mail us at:

Daphne Elementary School
c/o Meghan Everette, 1st Grade
2307 Main Street
Daphne, Alabama 36526

If you have other questions, please email Mrs. Everette at meverette@bcbe.org and we'd be happy to tell you more. Thank you for helping our first-grade classes travel around the world this year!

Sincerely,

Bibliography

Bibliography of Resources

Avery, S. (2011, June 14). Mystery Skype—who could it be? *The Avery Bunch* [Blog post]. Retrieved from www.mravery.edublogs.org/2011/06/14/mystery/

Badura, C. (2012, January 10). "When are we gonna do that again?" *Comfortably 2.0* [Blog post]. Retrieved from www.craigbadura.com/2012/01/when-are-we-gonna-do-that-again.html

Blumengarten, J. (2013, March 1). *@cybraryman Read Across the States* [Video file]. Retrieved from www.youtube.com/watch?v=zxi71A_lvME

Framework for 21st Century Learning. (2011, March). The Partnership for 21st Century Skills. Retrieved from www.p21.org/our-work/p21-framework

Graham, J. (2014, February 3). Super Bowl ad for Microsoft features Irvine classroom. *The Orange County Register*. Retrieved from www.ocregister.com/articles/bedley-600029-students-microsoft.html

Hart, T. (2014, February 19). 1st Mystery Skype! *Resources from the "Hart"* [Blog post]. Retrieved from http://blogs.henrico.k12.va.us/trhart/2014/02/19/1st-mystery-skype/

Kemp, C. (2014, November 16). What is Mystery Skype? 7 steps to get started! *Mr Kemp* [Blog post]. Retrieved from www.mrkempnz.com/2014/11/what-is-mystery-skype-8-steps-to-get-started.html

Krakower, B. (2013, February 20). Connecting beyond the school walls: Mystery Location Call. *Billy Krakower* [Blog post]. Retrieved from www.billykrakower.com/blog/connecting-beyond-the-school-walls-mystery-location-call

Miller, G. (2013, April 18). Try a Mystery Skype: Here's why. *Educational Leadership in the 21st Century* [Blog post]. Retrieved from www.gregmillerprincipal.com/2013/04/18/try-a-mystery-skype-heres-why/

#MysterySkype. *Skype in the classroom* [Website]. Retrieved from https://education.skype.com/mysteryskype

Ripp, P. (2013, February). Where in the world are they? Students find out with Mystery Skype. *Leading and Learning, 40* (5), 30–31. Retrieved from www.learningandleading-digital.com/learning_leading/201302#pg32

Scholastic Teachers. (2015). Making connections with Flat Stanley: Framed in France. *Scholastic.com*. Retrieved from www.scholastic.com/teachers/top-teaching/2014/10/making-connections-flat-stanley-framed-france

Skype in the classroom. (n.d.) *Projects*. [Website]. Retrieved from https://education.skype.com

Solarz, P. (2014, August). How to set up and run a Mystery Skype session. *What's Going on in Mr. Solarz' Class?* [Blog post]. Retrieved from www.psolarz.weebly.com/how-to-set-up-and-run-a-mystery-skype-session.html

Tolisano, S. (2014, May 10). Be the fly on the wall: Mystery Skype. *Langwitches Blog* [Blog post]. Retrieved from www.langwitches.org/blog/2014/05/10/be-the-fly-on-the-wall-mystery-skype/

Wiebe, G. (2013, December 3). Tip of the week: Mystery Skype. *History Tech* [Blog post]. Retrieved from www.historytech.wordpress.com/2013/12/06/tip-of-the-week-mystery-skype/

Yollis, L. (2011, June 8). Mystery Skype Call with Langwitches! *Mrs. Yollis' Classroom Blog* [Blog post]. Retrieved from www.yollisclassblog.blogspot.com/2011/06/mystery-skype-call-with-langwitches.html

Yollis, L. (2011, July 20). Langwitches' video of the Mystery Skype Call. *Mrs. Yollis' Classroom Blog* [Blog post]. Retrieved from www.yollisclassblog.blogspot.com/2011/07/langwitches-video-of-mystery-skype-call.html

Online Resources

Castles Northern Ireland, Virtual Visit Tours: www.virtualvisittours.com/category/castles-northern-ireland/

Connected Classrooms Workshop on Google+: https://plus.google.com/u/0/communities/100662407427957932931

Dan, Dan the Science Man:

www.dandanscienceman.com
www.dandanscienceman.com/scientists-help-science-teachers-using-social-media/
www.dandanscienceman.com/sci-u-share/

DreamWakers: www.dreamwakers.org/

Twitter Handles of Bibliography Sources

@pernilleripp (P. Ripp)
@mr_avery (S. Avery)
@PaulSolarz (P. Solarz)
@trockr11 (T. Hart)
@langwitches (S. Tolisano)
@lindayollis (L. Yollis)